SPOTLIGHT ON SPELLING

A structured guide to the assessment
and teaching of spelling

by

Claire Cootes and Juliet Jamieson

First Edition

ALPHABET BOOKS

Published by Alphabet Books, a division of The Alphabet Children Ltd, P.O. Box 75, Colchester, CO3 4JS

Cover design by Rory O'Brine
Illustrations by Angela Carless
Computer typeset by SB Datagraphics Ltd. Colchester
Printed in Great Britain by Anchor Brendon Ltd, Tiptree

ISBN 0-948280-01-8

British Library Cataloguing in Publication Data
Cootes Claire Spotlight on Spelling: a structural guide to the assessment and teaching of spelling. 1. English Language – Orthography and spelling – Study and teaching 1. Title   11 Jamieson, Juliet   428.1   PE1143
ISBN 0-948280-01-8

CONTENTS

CONTENTS continued.

FOREWORD

BY JAMES STEVENSON M.A.,M.Sc.

It gives me great pleasure to write a foreword to this new book on the teaching of spelling.

Some time ago, it became apparent that existing remedial programmes were not effective for many children, especially in view of the lengthy time it took to achieve any significant results.

I therefore suggested to Claire Cootes and Juliet Jamieson that they try a new approach and develop a scheme for the remedial teaching of spelling using intensive teaching methods. Over the past five years, these two experienced teachers have been using and developing a new, highly structured intensive scheme and have obtained excellent results.

The new method has become so effective that it seemed appropriate to make it readily available to others. The publication of this book meets this objective and enables teachers and parents to understand and teach spelling by this new means. The scheme represents a major advance and is proving successful with both children and adults of many varied ages and differing academic abilities.

Having referred many pupils to the authors and observed the development of this method at close hand, I am delighted with the results.

INTRODUCTION

Spotlight on Spelling has been designed for parents and teachers to provide a comprehensive and consistent guide to the assessment and teaching of spelling. Spotlight is a flexible scheme that will enable diagnosis of an individual's difficulties and the planning of an appropriate remedial programme.
Our experience in giving specialist tuition has convinced us of the need for such a guide.

Children of all ages who are under-achieving in reading, writing and spelling skills are referred to us by educational psychologists. The children are withdrawn from school for up to three weeks. They are given intensive individual tuition on the written language. We found that many of the children we taught had specific learning difficulties such as dyslexia often characterized by poor short term auditory or visual memory. Unfortunately these factors result in a discrepancy between general intelligence and academic performance in areas where literacy is vital.

Many children have environmental problems, such as limited or no access to reading or writing materials, these children may also be referred for tuition. We are aware that poor performance is not necessarily associated with low intelligence.

Bilingual children or children who are exposed to more than one language often need help, only the most linguistically able child can absorb the written structure of two languages simultaneously.

To provide a consistent remedial spelling programme we felt that it was necessary to establish a clear categorisation of spelling. We have listed the consonant and vowel sounds of the language and given examples of the various ways each sound can be spelt.

Our experience has also shown that spelling errors are frequently visual rather than auditory. Common errors are reversals such as the b/d or p/q confusion, directional; "tac" for "cat" or letter order, "lihgt" for "light". Many of these errors can be sorted out through auditory training, sound sequencing and careful monitoring of the written word. The use of colour and pictures, for example; "a goat in a coat in a boat" (to reinforce the "oa" spelling of the long "o" sound) are all invaluable teaching aids and should be incorporated in the "spelling programme" wherever possible. By learning groups of words with similar spelling patterns the child soon begins to know when a word "looks" right.

Spotlight can be used purely as a spelling reference book. The word lists in the **Spelling Programme** provide a useful reference for school teachers, teachers of English as a foreign or second language, poor spellers and their parents.

NOTE
This scheme covers the spelling of over 4,250 different words. It is therefore a highly comprehensive scheme.

PHONETIC SYMBOLS

Short Vowels

/ɪ/	ink	*
/ɛ/	egg	*
/æ/	apple	*
/ɒ/	orange	*
/ʊ/	book	*
/ʌ/	umbrella	*
/ə/	ever	

Long Vowels

/i/	eel	*			
/ɑ/	arm	*	/ɔɪ/	boy	*
/ɔ/	unicorn	*	/ɪə/	fear	
/u/	shoe	*	/ɛə/	where	
/ɜ/	church	*	/ʊə/	tour	
/eɪ/	ape	*	/ju/	unicorn	*
/əʊ/	note	*	/jʊə/	pure	
/aɪ/	ice cream	*	/aɪə/	fire	
/ɑʊ/	mouse	*	/ɑʊə/	hour	

Consonants

/p/	pig	*	/ð/	then		/ts/	schizoid	
/b/	boat	*	/s/	sun	*	/ks/	box	*
/t/	ten	*	/z/	zebra	*	/gz/	exam	*
/d/	dog	*	/ʃ/	shoe	*	/l/	lemon	*
/k/	kite	*	/ʒ/	measure		/w/	watch	*
/g/	goat	*	/f/	fish	*	/j/	yacht	*
/m/	mouse	*	/v/	van	*	/r/	rabbit	*
/n/	net	*	/h/	hat	*			
/ŋ/	wing	*	/tʃ/	church	*			
/θ/	three	*	/dʒ/	jug	*			

Symbols marked with an asterisk (*) are illustrated on pages 6 and 7

6

SHORT VOWELS	LONG VOWELS	DIPTHONGS

/ɪ/	/i/	/eɪ/
/ɛ/	/ɑ/	/əʊ/
/æ/	/ɔ/	/aɪ/
/ɒ/	/u/	/aʊ/
/ʊ/	/ɜ/	/ɔɪ/
/ʌ/		/ju/

Continue to refer to the illustrations when teaching these sounds to the pupil

CONSONANTS

/p/ /ŋ/ /tʃ/

/b/ /θ/ /dʒ/

/t/ /s/ /ks/

/d/ /z/ /gz/

/k/ /ʃ/ /l/

/g/ /f/ /w/

/m/ /v/ /j/

/n/ /h/ /r/

Continue to refer to the illustrations when teaching these sounds to the pupil

UNDERSTANDING OF BASIC PHONETICS

Although we are constrained in written language by the 26 letters of the alphabet, the sounds they represent are infinitely more complex. For example it is a commonly held view that there are 5 vowels. There are 5 vowel **letters** but our spoken language contains many more vowel **sounds**. For the purposes of this programme we have isolated 24 vowel sounds.

It is therefore essential to be able to differentiate between letters and sounds. It is also vital to be aware of the distinction between vowel sounds and consonant sounds.

CONSONANT SOUNDS: These are the speech sounds made when an obstruction in the mouth makes a barrier to the air stream. For example, the /b/ sound is made when the lips come together and the /f/ sound is made when the top teeth and the bottom lip make contact.

VOWEL SOUNDS: These sounds are made by altering the position of the tongue and lips, but unlike consonants there is never a complete obstruction to the air stream. For example, to make the /i/ sound in **fee**t the tongue must be close to the roof of the mouth at the front but to make the /ɑ/ sound in **yard** the mouth opens wide and the back of the tongue is only slightly arched towards the roof of the mouth.

CONSONANTS

Consonants are classified according to the presence or absence of voicing and the manner and place of articulation.

1. *VOICING*

Voiced sounds are characterised by the vibration of the vocal cords. The voiceless sounds have a whispered quality as there is no vibration of the vocal cords. For example the only difference between /b/ and /p/ is that /b/ is voiced and /p/ is voiceless, otherwise they are both formed in the same way, by making a barrier to the air stream with the lips.

VOICED SOUNDS	VOICELESS SOUNDS
/b/ /d/ /g/	/p/ /t/ /k/
/v/ /z/ /ʒ/ /ð/	/f/ /s/ /ʃ/ /θ/ /h/
/dʒ/	/tʃ/
/m/ /n/ /ŋ/	
/w/ /r/ /l/ /j/	

NB /ʒ/ as in measure, /ð/ as in **th**an, /ʃ/ as in **sh**ed
/θ/ as in **th**ink, /dʒ/ as in **j**ump, /tʃ/ as in **ch**ip
/ŋ/ as in bri**ng**, /j/ as in **y**ellow

8

2. *MANNER OF ARTICULATION*

Consonants are made by the tongue or lips making an obstruction to the air stream. This may be a complete obstruction as for /b/ when the lips close tightly together or a partial obstruction where air can still escape, for example, to make the /f/ sound the top teeth make contact with the lower lip but the air is still able to escape. To make the /m/ /n/ and /ŋ/ (bri**ng**) sounds the air passes through the nose. Consonant sounds are grouped in the following way:-

(a) *PLOSIVES:* These sounds have a complete obstruction of the air stream, the air pressure builds up behind the barrier which is suddenly released making an explosion of sound.

VOICED PLOSIVES	VOICELESS PLOSIVES
/b/ /d/ /g/	/p/ /t/ /k/

(b) *NASALS:* These sounds have an obstruction in the mouth but they allow the air to escape through the nose. They are all voiced.

VOICED NASALS

/m/ /n/ /ŋ/

(c) *FRICATIVES:* These sounds have only a partial obstruction to the air stream and as the air escapes through a narrow space the air becomes turbulent causing friction.

VOICED FRICATIVES	VOICELESS FRICATIVES
/v/ /z/ /ʒ/ /ð/	/f/ /s/ /ʃ/ /h/ /θ/

(d) *FRICTIONLESS CONTINUANTS:* These sounds are made when the barrier is not close enough to cause friction.

VOICED FRICTIONLESS CONTINUANTS

/w/ /r/ /l/ /j/

(e) *AFFRICATES:* These sounds are the combination of a plosive followed by a fricative. When the air is released to make the plosive sound a partial barrier remains causing friction of the airstream.

VOICED AFFRICATE	VOICELESS AFFRICATE
/dʒ/	/tʃ/

3. PLACE OF ARTICULATION

The obstruction of the air flow can be made by the lips teeth and tongue in the following positions:-

(a) bilabial (both lips brought together)

/p/ /b/ /m/ /w/

(b) labiodental (lower lip and top front teeth brought together)

/θ/ /ð/ /f/ /v/

(c) alveolar (front of the tongue and the ridge behind the top teeth brought together)

/t/ /d/ /ʃ/ /z/ /ʒ/ /s/

/dʒ/ /tʃ/ /n/ /l/ /r/

(d) velar (back of the tongue and the back of the palate brought together

/k/ /g/ /ŋ/

(e) glottal (the vocal cords)

/h/ (the air flow causes slight friction as it passes through the half open cords.)

VOWELS

The distinctive feature between vowels and consonants is that the production of vowel sounds does not involve any obstruction of the air stream in the mouth. Vowel sounds are always voiced (vibration of the vocal cords).

The quality of the vowel sound is dependent on the position of the tongue and the presence or absence of lip rounding.

To produce vowel sounds the front, centre, or back of the tongue will be raised towards the palate. The degree of jaw opening will determine how close the tongue is to the palate.

When the jaws are slightly apart a "**close**" vowel sound is produced (the tongue is "**close**" to the palate). When the jaws are further apart an "**open**" vowel is produced.

Thus	**Front** (ie front of the tongue raised)	**Central**	**Back**
Close	/i/ feet	/aʊ/ clown	/u/ do
Open	/æ/ sad	/ʌ/ mug	/ɑ/ yard

The following vowels have lip rounding:

/ɔ/ born
/ʊ/ book
/u/ do

There are three types of vowels: monophtongs diphthongs and triphthongs.

1. *Monophthongs*

Monophthongs are vowel sounds where the tongue and lips remain in the same position throughout the production of the sound. For example:

/i/ feet
/æ/ sad
/ʌ/ mug

2. *Diphthongs*

Diphthongs are vowel sounds where the tongue and/or lips glide from one position to another. For example:

/eɪ/ make
/əʊ/ note
/ɑʊ/ clown

3. *Triphthongs*

Triphthongs are vowel sounds where the tongue and/or lips change position twice before completion. For example:

/aɪə/ fire
/ɑʊə/ hour

NOTE: "Spotlight" is based on **Received Pronunciation**. Received Pronunciation is the English accent taught throughout the world. It is spoken throughout the British Isles but is predominantly associated with the South East of England. Our experience has shown that the scheme can be easily adapted to other accents.

INTRODUCING THE PUPIL TO PHONETICS

It is essential that the pupil has a grasp of the principles of phonetics so the spelling programme is both logical and meaningful to him. As the programme is auditory in its basis, listening skills are of particular importance.

It is important that the pupil can differentiate between letters and sounds. He will need to name all the letters of the alphabet in the usual way – a, b, c, etc. and then say what sounds each letter can make. At this stage, he can be introduced to the fact that one letter can make more than one sound and may already be aware, for example, that the letter c can be "hard" as in cake(/**k**/) or "soft" as in face (/**s**/).

VOICING

Even very young children can be taught to differentiate between voiced and voiceless sounds. By placing the fingers on the throat and articulating, for example a /**v**/ sound, vibration will be felt. As soon as voicing stops as in /**f**/, vibration ceases. The child is then encouraged to experiment with different sounds and he is soon able to distinguish this feature. Then the teacher can produce sounds at random and the pupil says whether they are voiced or voiceless. This distinction is important because in so many cases the only difference between the pronunciation of pairs of words lies in the feature of voicing. For example, bit & pit, van & fan, bad & pat, cot & god.

THE DISTINCTION BETWEEN VOWEL AND CONSONANT SOUNDS.

The pupil may be asked to articulate any sustained vowel sound such as /**ɑ**/ in car. First he will discover that the sound is voiced, and it will then be explained that all vowel sounds are voiced. He may then try some others to test this.

The child will experience the fact that there is no obstruction in the mouth when vowel sounds are produced. This notion can be explained by saying that vowel sounds "come out of your mouth easily". For this reason the vowel sounds are essential in speech. Children have often been taught that there is "a vowel in every word". This idea will now be clarified - there is at **least** one vowel **sound** in every word. At this point it is a good idea to write the child's name and address leaving out all the vowel letters (and y where appropriate). The pupil is then asked to read this aloud. It is almost impossible to do so without inserting vowel sounds.

12

ASSESSMENT AND TEACHING PROCEDURE

DIAGNOSTIC ASSESSMENT LIST

The Diagnostic Assessment list is the nucleus of the scheme. If used in the following way, it will lead the teacher directly to the appropriate section of the Spelling Programme.

HOW IT WAS DEVISED

The sounds of English can be written in many different ways. For example the /æ/ sound in cat can be written 'a' or 'ai' (as in the word "plait").

Other examples are:

/**p**/ has only one spelling 'p'
but /**k**/ can be spelt in 7 different ways:

c - **c**lap
k - ban**k**
ck - bla**ck**
final c - magi**c**
ch - a**ch**e
que - grotes**que**
cc - a**cc**ount
qu - **qu**ay

The assessment list simply consists of an example of most spelling forms in order of difficulty. All the speech sounds and the various ways they can be spelt can be found in the vowel and consonant reference lists. The Diagnostic Assessment list also includes examples of words where spelling is influenced by grammatical changes. For example: past tense endings, plurals, prefixes and suffixes. These words can be found in the grammatical reference list.

HOW TO USE THE ASSESSMENT LIST

Use with individual pupils.

Find an appropriate starting point. Ideally the starting point should be gauged so that less than 10 and more than 2 words are spelt correctly. A rough guideline as to Spelling Age (based on the Jamieson Diagnostic Spelling Test) is given at the beginning of each group of 10 words on the Assessment List.

The Assessment List should never be given as a complete Spelling Test. As soon as an error is made, stop and teach that spelling pattern. Beside each word there is

13

a reference to direct the teacher to the appropriate place in the spelling programme. The anticipated error (which is in heavy print) may not be made, if the pupil makes a different mistake it is necessary to refer back to the reference lists for the correct page of the Spelling Programme. Used in this way it has the great psychological advantage that the pupil immediately sees the relevance of what is being taught. Any lack of confidence when a pupil is writing a word, or any indication in free writing that a spelling is not fully known, should be further investigated.

THE SPELLING PROGRAMME

BEFORE IT CAN BE USED

Before the spelling programme can be used, it is necessary for the pupil to be aware of basic phonetic principles. He must be able to discriminate between vowel and consonant sounds and have an understanding of their distinctive features. For example, the idea that the vowel sounds are simply the letters "A, E, I, O, U" is not an adequate understanding of the true nature of vowel sounds. Children always find practical phonetics at this elementary level both interesting and enjoyable. Even young children can be made aware of how speech sounds are made. They can distinguish voiced and voiceless sounds by placing their fingers on their throat. Vibration of the vocal cords can be felt during a voiced sound such as /z/ and its absence noticed during voiceless sounds such as /s/. They can be taught to recognise the significance of the position of the lips, teeth and tongue in making individual speech sounds.

Often, throughout the spelling programme it is necessary to refer to phonetic terms, such as: vowels, consonants and voicing, in order to explain spelling patterns. It is for this reason that we feel it is important to devote a certain amount of time to teaching these basic concepts.

THE FORMAT OF THE SPELLING PROGRAMME

The Spelling Programme is the remedial section of the book. When an error is made in the Diagnostic Assessment List and the teacher has turned to the appropriate page in the Spelling Programme, he will find a word list which serves to reinforce the particular spelling pattern. Where appropriate there will be an explanation of the spelling rule. There are also sample dictations or exercises given for each spelling. Longer passages of dictation are listed at the back of the book, primarily for the more advanced levels, with an approximate level relating to the Diagnostic Assessment List.

The word lists are by no means exhaustive, especially in the more common terms. The frequency or rarity of a particular spelling pattern is self evident from the number of words which appear with each example in the Spelling Programme. As far as possible we have avoided listing the less frequent terms as "exceptions" in this scheme, taking the view that this complicates rather than clarifies. After each sound section, lists of homophones (words that sound the same but have different spellings and different meanings) are given.

USING THE SPELLING PROGRAMME

The words are listed alphabetically, rather than in order of difficulty, for ease of reference and so the teacher must select the words for dictation and practise which are suitable for each particular pupil. The pupil should be shown the written form and be taught to relate it to the speech sound in an active way. By grouping together words that look alike and by frequent use of colour and pictures the vital aspect of the visual skills involved in spelling is reinforced. The word lists should not simply be copied but dictated and elicited from the child himself.

FURTHER IDEAS FOR USING THE SPELLING PROGRAMME

(1) Ask pupils to use particular words in their own sentences.

(2) By using as many words of a particular spelling pattern as possible in a short paragraph, the pupils can make up "nonsense" stories. These can then be illustrated by the pupil. For example:

"Two knights were fighting in the moonlight . . ."

(3) Tell the pupil a story which contains several examples of a spelling form and ask the child to reproduce it.

(4) Show the pupil a picture which illustrates the target spelling form and ask him to write out as many of these as he can find. For example the picture might show a badger on a bridge eating fudge.

(5) Picture or word clue crosswords can be devised.

(6) Anagrams of words can be given for the pupils to solve.

(7) A long word may be given from which the pupil tries to find as many smaller words as possible which have a particular spelling pattern.

For example — How many "igh" words are there in

Nightmares

(8) Instead of simply dictating word lists, first read the list to the pupil then show it to him for a minute, close the book and ask him to write down all the words he remembers.

(9) Use the work book available from Alphabet Books and written by the authors (ISBN 0-948280-03-4).

Vowel Reference List

Vowel Reference List
Continued

Vowel Reference List
Continued
Page

Consonant Reference List

Consonant Reference List
Continued

Initial Consonant Blends

Page

1	sp	113
2	st	113
3	sm	113
4	sn	113
5	sl	113
6	sw	113
7	sc	113
8	sk	113
9	spl	113
10	spr	113
11	scr	113
12	str	113
13	shr	114
14	tr	114
15	tw	114
16	dr	114
17	dw	114
18	pl	114
19	pr	114
20	br	114
21	bl	114
22	cl	115
23	cr	115
24	gl	115
25	gr	115
26	fl	115
27	fr	115
27	thr	115

Final Consonant Blends

Page

1	st	116
2	sk	116
3	sp	116
4	nk	116
5	nd	116
6	nt	116
7	nch	116
8	mp	116
9	ct	116
10	ft	117
11	lk	117
12	lp	117
13	ld	117
14	thm	117
15	sm	117
16	xt	117

Morphological/
Grammatical Reference

Morphological/ Grammatical Reference

Page

Prefixes

Suffixes

N.B.   C = consonant   V = vowel $\bar{V}$ = long vowel $\dot{V}$ = short vowel

Endings

Stress

Diagnostic Assessment Lists

suff = suffix   pre = prefix
pl = plural   Adv = adverb
FB = word final blend   IB = word initial blend
VB cont = continuous form of the verb
VB past = past form of the verb
end = ending

			Page				Page
1: 5 yrs				**4: 6.3 yrs**			
sad	/æ/ /s/		37,95	moon	/u/		47
ten	/ɛ/ /t/		35,80	quit	/kw/		87
pig	/ɪ/ /p/		33,79	low	/əʊ/		62,108
box	/ɒ/ /ks/		40,106	fly	/aɪ/		65
mug	/ʌ/ /g/		50,86	flight	/aɪ/		66
spin	IB		113	sniff	/f/		93
plum	IB		114	dwell	/l/		108
clap	IB, /k/		83,115	dress	/s/		95
gift	FB		117	black	/k/		84
jump	FB /dʒ/		116	born	/ɔ/		42
2: 5.3 yrs				**5: 7 yrs**			
shed	/ʃ/		99	find	/aɪ/		66
chip	/tʃ/		103	boy	/ɔɪ/		69
then	/ð/		94	pie	/aɪ/		66
bring	/ŋ/		91	bird	/ɜ/		51
bank	/ŋ/		91	drinking	vb cont		122
spring	IB		113	book	/ʊ/		46
think	/θ/		94	two	/u/		48
lunch	FB		116	ball	/ɔ/		42
thrush	IB /ʃ/		115	army	/ɑ/ /i/		30
make	/eɪ/		58,88	want	/ɒ/ /w/		40,111
3: 6 yrs				**6: 7.6 yrs**			
do	/u/ /d/		47,82	pull	/ʊ/		46
note	/əʊ/ /n/		61,89	fast	/ɑ/		38
yard	/ɑ/ /j/		38,112	key	/i/		30
kite	/aɪ/ /k/		65,83	coin	/ɔɪ/		70
cube	/ju/		74	have	/v/		94
feet	/i/ /f/		29,92	path	/ɑ/		39
heat	/i/ /h/		29,102	taking	vb cont.		123
train	/eɪ/		58	swimming	vb cont		124
boat	/əʊ/ /b/		61	clown	/aʊ/		68
way	/eɪ/		59	carrying	vb cont		124

Diagnostic Assessment Lists

7: **8 yrs**		*Page*	10: **9.3 yrs**		*Page*
zoo	/z/	97	lik**ed**	vb past	119
house	/aʊ/ /s/	68,95	fad**ed**	vb past	120
agr**eeing**	vb cont	125	ho**pped**	vb past,suff.	120,135
ty**ing**	vb cont	125	hurr**ied**	vb past	121
come	/ʌ/	50	slep**t**	vb past	121
a**dd**	/d/	82	**c**y**c**le	/s/ /l/	96,109
e**gg**	/g/	86	**wh**ole	/h/	102
bri**dg**e	/dʒ/	104	ma**g**i**c**	/dʒ /k/	105,84
fe**r**n	/ɜ/	52	**g**uilty	/g/	86
d**ye**	/aɪ/	67	**sw**arm	/ɔ/	43

8: **8.6 yrs**			11: **9.6 yrs**		
ca**tch**	/tʃ/	103	w**or**ld	/ɜ/	53
r**oll**	/əʊ/ /r/	62	m**a**ny	/ɛ/	36
f**ew**	/ju/	75	b**u**ry	/ɛ/	36
b**uy**	/aɪ/	67	s**ai**d	/ɛ/	36
where	/ɛə/ /w/	72,111	cl**aw**	/ɔ/	43
p**ure**	/jʊə/	76	w**a**lk	/ɔ/	43
t**oe**	/əʊ/	63	th**eir**	/ɛə/	72
s**ore**	/ɔ/	42	**t**une	/tʃ/	103
fl**oor**	/ɔ/	43	fri**e**nd	/ɛ/	36
h**ea**d	/ɛ/	35	h**a**lf	/ɑ/	39

9: **9 yrs**			12: **10 yrs**		
n**ur**se	/ɜ/	52	m**u**sic	/ju/	75
fr**o**nt	/ʌ/	50	bl**ue**	/u/	48
ch**air**	/ɛə/	72	scr**ew**	/u/	48
ev**er**	/ə/	54	**gh**ost	/g/	87
wait**ed**	vb past	118	st**ea**k	/eɪ/	59
sav**ed**	vb past	118	sh**oes**	/u/ /z/ pl	48,98,126
fi**ng**er	/ŋg/	92	f**ear**	/ɪə/	70
wonder**ful**	suff	140	box**es**	pl	126
play**ed**	vb past	119	wolv**es**	pl	127
help**ed**	vb past	119	church**es**	pl	126

Diagnostic Assessment Lists

13: **10.3 yrs**			Page		16: **11.3 yrs**			Page
duties	/dʒ/		105		diary	/aɪə/		76
pianos	/əʊ/	pl	63,128		hour	/aʊə/		77
tomatoes	pl		128		through	/u/		48
field	/i/		31		heart	/ɑ/		39
court	/ɔ/		44		bear	/ɛə/		73
young	/ʌ/		51		soup	/u/		49
ceiling	/i/		31		shone	/ɒ/		41
roar	/ɔ/		44		grey	/eɪ/		59
quickly	adv		129		truth	/u/		49
poor	/ʊə/		74		include	/u/		49

14: **10.6. yrs**					17: **11.6 yrs**			
athlete	/i/		31		sure	/ʊə/ /ʃ/		74,99
happen	/n/		89		power	/aʊə/		77
lovely	adv suff		129,137		people	/i/		31
lazily	adv		130		fruit	/u/		49
simply	adv		130		tour	/ʊə/		74
fatally	adv		131		climb	/m/		88
historically	adv		131		autumn	/ɔ/ /m/		44,88
expand	/ks/		106		operation	/ʃ/		99
does	/ʌ/		51		choose	/z/		98
exact	/gz/		107		animal	/l/		109

15: **11 yrs**					18: **12 yrs**			
rare	/ɛə/		72		phone	/f/		93
deer	/ɪə/		70		leisure	/ɛ/		36
dragon	/n/		89		either	/aɪ/		67
organ	/n/		90		ache	/k/		85
knife	/n/		90		horrible	end		141
could	/ʊ/		46		honest	/ɑ/		41
fire	/aɪə/		76		cellar	/ə/		54
earth	/ɜ/		53		listen	/s/		96
though	/əʊ/		63		capable	end		141
caught	/ɔ/		44		myth	/ɪ/		33

Diagnostic Assessment Lists

		Page				Page
19: 12.3 yrs			**22: 13 yrs**			
sword	/s/	96	device	/s/		96
pretty	/ɪ/	34	matt	/t/		81
straight	/eɪ/	59	leopard	/ɛ/		36
forbidden	stress	145	wrist	/r/		110
busy	/ɪ/	34	brewery	end		141
build	/ɪ/	34	lazily	suff		138
visitor	/ə/	54	freight	/eɪ/		60
bargain	/n/	90	Thames	/t/		81
traveller	stress	145	indistinct	pre		133
women	/ɪ/	34	doubt	/t/		81
20: 12.6 yrs			**23: 13.3 yrs**			
status	/ə/	55	possess	/z/		98
brought	/ɔ/	45	plough	/aʊ/		69
acre	/ə/	55	opinion	/j/		112
veil	/eɪ/	59	impudent	end		142
modern	/n/	90	informant	end		142
harbour	/ə/	55	hindrance	end		142
mere	/ɪə/	71	cough	/ɒ/ /f/		41,93
ridiculous	/ə/	56	independence	end		142
weird	/ɪə/	71	laugh	/ɑ/		39
lyre	/aɪə/	76	science	/s/		97
21: 12.9 yrs			**24: 13.6 yrs**			
choir	/aɪə/ /kw/	77,87	gnaw	/n/		90
discomfort	pre	132	picture	/tʃ/		103
fiery	/aɪə/	77	measure	/ʒ/		101
forehead	pre	132	mayor	/ɛə/		73
misfortune	pre	132	dial	/aɪ/		67
pier	/ɪə/	71	prayer	/ɛə/		73
forgo	pre	133	tongue	/ŋ/		91
dissemble	pre	132	singeing	vb cont		125
grotesque	/k/	85	question	/tʃ/		104
advise	/z/	98	television	/ʒ/		101

Diagnostic Assessment Lists

			Page
25:	**13.9 yrs**		
	partial	/ʃ/	100
	ancient	/ʃ/	100
	Austria	/ɒ/	41
	rhino	/r/	110
	mission	/ʃ/	100
	account	/k/	85
	exhaust	/ɔ/	45
	exhibit	/ɪ/	34
	adjective	/dʒ/	105
	pension	/ʃ/	100
26:	**14 yrs**		
	temporary	end	143
	brochure	/ʃ/	100
	crises	pl	128
	ocean	/ʃ/	101
	precarious	/ə/	56
	irregular	pre	134
	prestige	/ʒ/	102
	sergeant	/ɑ/	39
	shoulder	/əʊ/	64
	acquire	/kw/	87
27:	**14.3 yrs**		
	instantaneous	/ə/	56
	murmur	/ə/	57
	thorough	/ə/	57
	quay	/k/ /i/	32,85
	violent	/aɪə/	77
	adequate	/ə/	57
	compulsory	end	143
	aeroplane	/ɛə/	73
	journey	/ɜ/	53
	prosperity	end	143

			Page
28:	**14.6 yrs**		
	exception	/ks/	107
	route	/u/	49
	queue	/ju/	75
	inertia	/ə/	57
	specify	end	143
	theory	/ɪə/	71
	accessible	/ks/	107
	yeoman	/əʊ/	64
	psalm	/s/	97
	conscious	/ʃ/	101
29:	**15 yrs**		
	picnicking	suff	139
	receipt	/t/	81
	liquefy	end	144
	plait	/æ/	37
	colonel	/ə/	53
	indict	/t/	81
	neutral	/ju/	75
	maestro	/aɪ/	67
	pneumonia	/n/	90
	anaemic	/i/	32
30:	**15.6 yrs**		
	xerox	/z/	98
	phoenix	/i/	32
	eyrie	/ɪə/	71
	seizure	/ʒ/	102
	gaelic	/eɪ/	60
	schizoid	/ts/	106
	mnemonic	/n/	91

THE SPELLING PROGRAMME VOWELS

The vowel sounds are listed in the order of the **Vowel Reference List**.

SECTION 1. /i/   SPELLING ALTERNATIVES

1 f**ee**t
2 h**ea**t
3 arm**y**
4 k**ey**
5 f**ie**ld
6 c**ei**ling
7 athl**ete**
8 p**eo**ple
9 qu**ay**
10 an**ae**mic
11 ph**oe**nix

1.1: /i/   *ee*   Test Word *feet*

agree	knee	speed
bee	meet	steel
creep	need	steep
deep	payee	street
exceed	queen	succeed
fee	seed	sweet
feel	seem	tee
feet	seen	teeth
flee	sheep	three
green	sheet	tree
heel	sleep	week
keep	speech	wheel

Note: he, she, we, be

Dictation

1. I can see a bee on the green tree.
2. The queen will make a speech next week.

1.2: /i/   *ea*   Test Word *heat*

beach	heat	scream
bean	lean	sea
beat	meal	seat
clean	mean	tea
cream	meat	teach
dream	neat	treat
eat	peace	weak
feast	read	wheat

Note: **ea-e**; breathe

29

Dictation

1. We had a feast on the beach by the sea.
2. It is a treat to eat lean meat for tea.

Fill in the blanks and use words in sentences.

h___, scr___, t__, cr___.

1.3: /i/   *y*   **Test Word army**

Final e is silent. /i/, when final, is usually written with a y.

any	easy	lazy
army	family	many
baby	fancy	only
body	funny	party
carry	greedy	penny
city	happy	pretty
clumsy	holy	ready
company	hurry	silly
country	jelly	stony
early	lady	worry

ly

gladly
happily
lovely
monthly
weekly

Dictation

1. The fancy lady went to a party in the city.
2. The greedy baby had jelly for tea.

Fill in the blanks and use the words in sentences.

onl_, slowl_, stor_, greed_.

1.4: /i/   *ey*   **Test Word key**

chimney	jockey	money
donkey	journey	monkey
hockey	key	parsley
honey	lackey	storey
		valley

Dictation

1. The jockey rode the donkey in the valley.
2. Where is the key to the monkey cage?

Fill in the blanks.

The smoke went up the ch_____.   We went on a long j_____.

1.5: /i/   *ie*   **Test Word f*i*eld**

brief	grieve	shriek
belief	niece	siege
chief	priest	shield
field	piece	thief
grief	relief	wield
	relieve	yield

Dictation

1. The priest said my niece was a thief.

Fill in the blanks and use the words in sentences.

p__ce, gr__f, sh__ld, rel__f.

1.6: /i/   *ei*   **Test Word c*ei*ling**
Always write ei after c.

caffeine	perceive
ceiling	protein
conceit	receipt
conceive	seize
deceit	seizure
deceive	

Dictation

1. He is very conceited and deceives people.
2. Meat has a lot of protein.

1.7: /i/   *eCV*   **Test Word athl*e*te**
(e + consonant and vowel)

abstemious	concede	impede
athlete	concrete	intercede
compete	extreme	recede
complete	facetious	theme

Dictation

1. Pete is a good athlete.
2. Concrete is extremely hard.

1.8: /i/   *eo*   **Test Word p*eo*ple**

people

Anagram - popeel, use the word in a sentence.

1.9: /i/   ay   Test Word qu*ay*

quay

Dictation

The boat left the quay.

1.10: /i/   ae   Test Word an*ae*mic

anaemia	caesar	leukaemia
anaemic	haemoglobin	paediatric

Dictation

1. I think he is anaemic.
2. We raised money for leukaemia.

1.11: /i/   oe   Test Word ph*oe*nix

amoeba	foetus	phoenix
coelacanth		

Homophones

beach	beech	steal	steel
bean	been	weak	week
feat	feet	tea	tee
flea	flee	peak	peek
heal	heel	read	reed
knead	need	peace	piece
leak	leek	key	quay
meat	meet	ceiling	sealing
peal	peel	scene	seen
sea	see	story	storey
seam	seem		

Fill in the blanks

The _____ trees were near the _____.   (beach, beech)
Where have you _____?   (bean, been)
The tap has a _____.   (leek, leak)
_____ me an orange please.   (peal, peel)
He went to ___ the ___.   (sea, see)
Last _____ I felt very _____.   (week, weak)

SECTION 2. /ɪ/　　　SPELLING ALTERNATIVES

1. p**i**g
2. m**y**th
3. pr**e**tty
4. b**u**sy
5. b**ui**ld
6. w**o**men
7. ex**hi**bit

2.1: /ɪ/　　　　*i*　　　**Test Word pig**

bid	hit	silk
big	inch	sing
bin	ink	sit
blink	is	slim
bring	jig	slip
chip	kid	snip
crisp	lid	spin
did	limp	sting
dig	lip	think
drink	mint	trip
fin	pig	twig
fist	pinch	twist
fit	pin	win
gin	rich	wind
grin	ring	wing
hid	ship	wit

Dictation

Dig a pit for the big pink pig.
The kid will sit on the bin lid.

2.2: /ɪ/　　　　*y*　　　**Test Word myth**

abysmal	mystery	syllable
abyss	myth	syllabus
crystal	oxygen	symbol
cygnet	paroxysm	symmetry
Egypt	physics	sympathy
gypsy	pygmy	symptom
hymn	pyramid	syrup
hypnosis	sycamore	system
		typical

Dictation

1. The gypsy read the myth about the pyramids in Egypt.
2. Sympathy has three syllables.
3. We learnt about crystals and oxygen in our physics syllabus.

Quiz

We need it to stay alive	O-----.
A tree	S-------.
A young swan	C-----.

2.3: /ɪ/   *e*   Test Word pr*e*tty

England   English   pretty

Dictation

A pretty English girl lived in England.

2.4: /ɪ/   *u*   Test Word b*u*sy

busily   business   busy

Dictation

The busy business man worked busily on his project.

2.5: /ɪ/   *ui*   Test Word b*ui*ld

biscuit	building	guild
build	built	guilt
		guilty (see/g/ 6:3)

Dictation

He built a building for making biscuits.
The man confessed his guilt.

2.6: /ɪ/   *o*   Test Word w*o*men

women

Dictation

There were three women in the play.

2.7: /ɪ/   *hi*   Test Word ex*hi*bit

exhibit   exhibition   exhilarate

Dictation

This is my exhibit for the exhibition.

Homophones

hymn	him
guilt	gilt

Dictation

He told him to sing the hymn.
He admitted his guilt.

SECTION 3. /ɛ/   SPELLING ALTERNATIVES

1. ten
2. head
3. many
4. bury
5. said
6. friend
7. leisure
8. leopard

3.1: /ɛ/   e   Test Word ten

bed	length	pet
bend	let	rest
bench	mend	sent
bet	met	set
get	nest	spend
jet	net	spent
leg	pest	wet

Dictation

1. Let the pet get on the bed.
2. We went for a rest on the bench.
3. The leg would not mend quickly.

3.2: /ɛ/   ea   Test Word head

already	health	read
bread	heather	ready
breast	heaven	spread
breath	heavy	steadily
dead	instead	steady
deaf	jealous	stealth
deafen	leather	sweat
death	lead	treasure
dreadful	meadow	thread
dreamt	meant	threat
feather	measure	wealth
head	pleasure	weather
		weapon

Dictation

Put the spread on the bread.
She put the feather hat on her head.

3.3: /ɛ/   *a*   **Test Word many**

any   many   Thames

Dictation

There are many boats on the Thames.

3.4: /ɛ/   *u*   **Test Word bury**

burial   bury

Dictation

The dog will bury the bone.

3.5: /ɛ/   *ai*   **Test Word said**

said

Dictation

John said he was going home.

3.6: /ɛ/   *ie*   **Test Word friend**

friend

Dictation

Tom is my best friend.

3.7: /ɛ/   *ei*   **Test Word leisure**

leisure   heifer

Dictation

He likes to go to the leisure centre.
A heifer is a young cow.

3.8: /ɛ/   *eo*   **Test Word leopard**

leopard

Anagram

eolprda = a wild cat.

Homophones

cell		sell
cent	scent	sent
check		cheque
lead		led
berry		bury

Fill in the Blanks

1. I must _____ that _____. (cheque, check)
2. He went to the prison _____. (cell, sell)
3. He _____ her some _____. (sent, scent)
4. The _____ in my pencil has broken. (lead, led)
5. The mouse _____ the _____. (berries, buries)

SECTION 4. /æ/   SPELLING ALTERNATIVES

1. s*a*d
2. pl*ai*t

4.1: /æ/   *a*   Test Word s*a*d

act	fat	sand
at	flag	sank
band	flash	sat
bank	gap	slap
bash	ham	snap
bat	hand	stamp
cat	jam	stand
crash	lamp	strap
Dad	mash	tap
dam	plan	thank
drag	pram	trap

Dictation

The fat cat sat at the tap.
Dad had jam on his hat.

4.2: /æ/   *ai*   Test Word pl*ai*t

plaid	plait

Dictation

She plaits her long hair.

SECTION 5. /ɑ/   SPELLING ALTERNATIVES

1. yard
2. fast
3. path
4. chance
5. half
6. heart
7. laugh
8. sergeant

5.1: /ɑ/   *ar*   Test Word *yard*

ark	farm	shark
arm	hard	sharp
bar	harm	smart
car	lard	spar
card	large	spark
charm	march	star
dark	mark	start
darn	part	tart
dart	scar	yard

Dictation

Park the car in the dark farm yard.
March in the park.
He had a scar on his arm.

5.2: /ɑ/   *a(s)*   Test Word *fast*

ask	clasp	mast
bask	fast	master
basket	fasten	nasty
blast	grasp	plaster
cast	last	rascal
castle	mask	task
		vast

5.3: /ɑ/   *a(n)*

dance
France
advance
chance

Dictation

Fasten the last rope to the mast.
The nasty master ran fast after the rascal.

5.4: /a/ *a(f/th)* Test Word **path**

aft	craft	raft
after	daft	rather
afterwards	father	shaft
bath	path	staff

Note: garage

Dictation

My father had a bath after making his path.

Quiz

Group of teachers = s_____.
A simple boat   = r_____.
Silly   = d_____.

5.5: /a/ *al* Test Word **half**

alms	embalm	psalm
calf	half	qualm
calm	palm	

Dictation

The calf was very calm.
We only sang half the psalm.
I cut the palm of my hand.

5.6: /a/ *ear* Test Word **heart**

heart	hearth

Quiz

Pumps blood around our bodies = h_____.
Part of a fireplace   = h_____.

5.7: /a/ *au* Test Word **laugh**

laugh	laughter	draught

Quiz

A cold current of air = d_____.
We all l_____ at the joke.

5.8: /a/ *er* Test Word **sergeant**

Berkshire	clerk	sergeant

Dictation

The sergeant sent the clerk to Berkshire.

SECTION 6. /ɒ/   SPELLING ALTERNATIVES

1. b**o**x
2. w**a**nt
3. sh**o**ne
4. h**o**nest
5. c**o**ugh
6. A**u**stria

6.1: /ɒ/   *o*   **Test Word box**

along	flop	not
blond	fog	plot
bond	got	pond
box	hot	pop
chop	job	rot
clog	jog	shop
cloth	log	smog
cod	long	song
cot	lost	stop
dog	lot	strong
drop	mop	

Dictation

The dog got hot.
He has not got a job.

6.2: /ɒ/   *(w)a*
                     (qu)a   **Test Word want**

a after w (or /**kw**/ making the /ɒ/ sound)

quad	swallow	was
squabble	swan	wash
squad	swap	wasp
squadron	wand	watch
squash	wander	what
squat	want	

Dictation

I want to watch the swan.
Was that a wasp?
The squadron played squash in the quad.

6.3: /ɒ/   *o(e)*   **Test Word sho*ne***

         gone   scone   shone

Dictation

Where has he gone?
The sun shone all day.

6.4: /ɒ/   *ho*   **Test Word *ho*nest**

         honest   honorary   honour
                                        hono(u)rable

Dictation

The honest boy never told lies.
She was made an honorary member of the club.

6.5: /ɒ/   *ou*   **Test Word c*ou*gh**

         cough   trough

Dictation

He had a bad cough.
The pigs food is in the trough.

6.6: /ɒ/   *au*   **Test Word *Au*stria**

         Australia   Austria   cauliflower
         sausage

Dictation

He ate sausages and cauliflower in Austria.

SECTION 7. /ɔ/   SPELLING ALTERNATIVES

        1. **b**orn
        2. **b**all
        3. **s**ore
        4. **fl**oor
        5. s**w**arm
        6. **cl**aw
        7. **w**alk
        8. **co**urt
        9. **r**oar
      10. **c**augh**t**
      11. **au**tumn
      12. **br**ough**t**
      13. exh**au**st

7.1: /ɔ/   *or*   **Test Word b*or*n**

born	forty	pork
cord	horn	port
corn	horse	short
corner	lord	snort
for	morning	sort
fork	nor	sport
form	north	stork
fort	or	storm
forth	porch	torn

Dictation

The Lord's horse was born in the morning.

Quiz

A knife and ____.
Opposite of South = _____.
Bad wind and rain = _____.

Note: *hor* exhort, exhortion

7.2: /ɔ/   *a(l)*   **Test Word b*all***

all	hall	small
ball	halt	stall
call	malt	tall
fall	salt	wall

Dictation

The wall in the hall was tall.
We all had a small ball.

7.3: /ɔ/   *ore*   **Test Word s*ore***

bore	lore	shore
core	more	sore
fore	ore	store
gore	pore	whore
		wore

Dictation

I got some more from the store.

Quiz

The sea _____.
A dull person   = _____.
The middle of an apple = _____.

7.4: /ɔ/ *oor* **Test Word floor**

door floor

Dictation

Close the door.
We put a rug on the floor.

7.5: /ɔ/ *(qu)/(w)ar* **Test Word swarm**

dwarf	swarm	warm
quart	towards	warp
quarter	war	wart
reward	ward	

Note: water

Dictation

The dwarf got a reward in the war.
The swarm went towards the water.

7.6: /ɔ/ *aw* **Test Word claw**

awful	flaw	saw
awkward	gnaw	shawl
bawl	law	straw
claw	lawn	thaw
draw	paw	yawn
dawn	raw	

Dictation

I saw the awful claws on the cat's paws.
The lawn looked like straw.

7.7: /ɔ/ *al* **Test Word walk**

chalk	stalk	talk
walk		

Dictation

We went for a walk and had a talk.

Quiz

Stem of a plant = s _____.
For writing on a blackboard = c_____.

7.8: /ɔ/ *our* **Test Word *court***

course	four	mourning
court	mourn	pour

Dictation

Four of us went on a tour of the court.
He is doing a difficult course at the university.
His father died so he is in mourning.

7.9: /ɔ/ *oar* **Test Word *roar***

board	coarse	oar
hoarse	roar	

Note: **oa** broad

Dictation

The oar was on board the boat.

7.10: /ɔ/ *augh* **Test Word *caught***

caught	fraught	slaughter
daughter	haughty	taught
distraught	naughty	

Dictation

He taught my naughty daughter.
He was very distraught when he heard the bad news.
The cattle were taken to the slaughter shed.
The cricketer caught the ball.

7.11: /ɔ/ *au* **Test Word *autumn***
(never at the end of a word)

auction	bauble	haunt
August	cause	launch
author	caution	laundry
auto	clause	Paul
autumn	fault	sauce
astronaut	haul	saucer
		saunter

Dictation

Paul was an author.
There was great caution for the astronauts' launch.

Quiz

A month	= _____
A place for cleaning clothes	= _____
A season	= _____

Fill in the Blank

A cup and _____.

7.12: /ɔ/   *ough*   Test Word br*ough*t

bought	nought	thought
brought	ought	wrought
fought	sought	

Dictation

I bought some wrought iron and brought it home.
I thought they fought all night.

7.13: /ɔ/   *hau*   Test Word ex*hau*st

exhaust

Dictation

We had to have the exhaust mended quickly.

Homophones

ball		bawl
board		bored
caught		court
course		coarse
fought		fort
four	for	fore
hall		haul
hoard		horde
oar	ore	or
pause		paws
pore		pour
sore	soar	saw
sought		sort

Dictation

He started to ____.	(ball, bawl)
We found out where to ____ the ship.	(board, bored)
The ____ looked very pretty with the new blue wallpaper.	(hall, haul)
The ____ on the cat were very large.	(pause, paws)
We saw the plane ____ in the air.	(sore, soar)

SECTION 8. /ʊ/   SPELLING ALTERNATIVES

1. book
2. pull
3. could

8.1: /ʊ/   *oo*   Test Word b*oo*k

book	good	rook
brook	hood	stood
cook	hook	took
crook	look	wood
foot	nook	wool

Dictation

The cook took a good look at her book.
He stood with one foot on the stool.

Quiz

A criminal _____. (rocok)
From trees _____. (owdo)

8.2: /ʊ/   *u*   Test Word p*u*ll

bull	full	pull
put		

Dictation

Pull the bull and put him in the barn.

Quiz

Opposite of empty = f ___.

8.3: /ʊ/   *oul*   Test Word c*oul*d

could	should	would

Dictation

He would like to go home.
She should have spoken clearly as they could not understand her.

SECTION 9. /u/   SPELLING ALTERNATIVES

1. do
2. moon
3. two
4. blue
5. screw
6. shoes
7. through
8. soup
9. truth
10. include
11. fruit
12. route

9.1: /u/   *o*   **Test Word do**

do   to   lose
who

Note: prove, move (final v must be followed by e)

Dictation

Who told you what to do?

9.2: /u/   *oo*   **Test Word moon**

boot	loom	spool
broom	mood	spoon
choose	moon	stool
cool	noon	too
droop	pool	tool
food	roof	tooth
fool	room	troop
gloom	school	zoom
groom	soon	

Dictation

The groom sat on a stool eating food with a spoon

QUIZ

Where we go to learn = sch _____.
Used to sweep the floor = br _____.
Shines at night = m _____.
Looks after horses = gr _____.

9.3: /u/   *wo*   **Test Word *two***

two

Dictation

The two cars went to London too quickly.

9.4: /u/   *ue*   **Test Word bl*ue***

accrue   clue   sue
blue   glue   true

Dictation

I had some blue glue.

Quiz

Opposite of false = ____.
The policeman found a ____ to the crime.

9.5: /u/   *ew*   **Test Word scr*ew***

blew   drew   jew
chew   flew   screw
crew   grew   strew
                                threw

Quiz

People working on the ship = ____.
Past of throw   = ____.
Past of blow   = ____.
Past of fly   = ____.
Past of grow   = ____.

9.6: /u/   *oe*   **Test Word sho*es***

canoe   shoe

Dictation

I left my shoes in the canoe.

9.7: /u/   *ough*   **Test Word thr*ough***

through

Dictation

He threw the ball through the window.

9.8: /u/   *ou*   **Test Word soup**

coupon	soup	you
group	wound	

Dictation

Will you give the group a soup coupon?

9.9: /u/   *u*   **Test Word truth**

Ruth	truth

Dictation

Ruth never tells the truth.

9.10: /u/   *u + vowel*   **Test Word include**

crude	intrude	recluse
delude	juvenile	rude
include		

Dictation

The crude juvenile was rude to the recluse.

9.11: /u/   *ui*   **Test Word fruit**

bruise	juice	sluice
cruise	pursuit	suit
fruit		

Dictation

We drank fruit juice on our cruise.
A man wears a suit.
She got a bruise on her knee when she fell.

9.12: /u/   *ou-e*   **Test Word route**

route	rouge

Dictation

Which route will you take to France?

SECTION 10. /ʌ/   SPELLING ALTERNATIVES

1. mug   4. young
2. come   5. does
3. front   6. blood

10.1: /ʌ/   *u*   Test Word m*u*g

blush	hush	pup
brush	hut	rut
bun	jump	slug
bunch	just	shut
bunk	lump	stung
but	lunch	sum
cup	lung	sun
cut	much	thrush
drunk	mug	trunk
fun	Mum	trust
grunt	nut	up
gun	plum	us
hunt	pump	

Dictation

The pup had fun in the hut.   Mum cut up a bun for us.

10.2: /ʌ/   *o-e*   Test Word c*ome*

above	dove	love
come	glove	none
done		some

Note: There is no such spelling as 'uv', ov must be used for the /ʌ/ sound

Dictation

Come and see some doves.

10.3: /ʌ/   *o*   Test Word fr*o*nt

among	honey	onion	
amongst	London	other	
another	Monday	oven	
brother	money	son	
cover	monkey	sponge	
discover	monk	ton	
dozen	month	tongue	
front	Mother	won	
govern	nothing	wonder	worry

Dictation

My mother and brother discovered some money in the oven.
I come to London one Monday a month.

10.4: /ʌ/   *ou*   Test Word *young*

country	flourish	touch
couple	nourish	tough
cousin	nourished	trouble
double	rough	young
enough		

Dictation

My young cousin got in trouble for touching the plug.
I've had enough of my tough rough cousin.

10.5: /ʌ/   *oe*   Test Word *does*

does

Dictation

Where does he live?

Homophones

none	nun
one	won
sun	son

10.6: /ʌ/   *oo*

blood   flood

SECTION 11. /ɜ/   SPELLING ALTERNATIVES

1. b**ir**d
2. f**er**n
3. n**ur**se
4. w**or**ld
5. **ear**th
6. jo**ur**ney
7. co**lo**nel

11.1: /ɜ/   *ir*   Test Word b**ir**d

bird	firm	skirt
birth	first	stir
circle	flirt	swirl
circus	girl	third
dirt	girth	thirteen
dirty	shirt	thirty
fir	sir	

Dictation

The girl got her skirt dirty.
The bird sat on the fir tree.
We see clowns at the circus.
There are thirty days in September.

11.2: /3/   *er*   **Test Word fern**

berth	herb	shepherd
certain	Perth	stern
expert	person	term
fern	serve	verb
		verse

Dictation

The stern shepherd went to Perth.

Quiz

Adds flavour to food.	h_____.
To wait on someone.	s_____.
An action word.	v_____.
Part of a poem.	v_____.

11.3: /3/   *ur*   **Test Word nurse**

burden	disturb	surface
burglar	further	surname
burn	hurl	surplus
burnt	hurt	surprise
burst	murder	survive
church	murmur	Thursday
curl	nurse	turkey
curse	purpose	urchin
curtain	purse	urge
curve	suburb	urgent

Quiz

1. A wound caused by fire.   b_____.
2. A popped balloon.   b_____.
3. You sing hymns there.   c_____.
4. You keep money in it.   p_____.
5. She works in a hospital.   n_____.
6. To throw wildly.   h____.
7. The fifth day of the week   Th_____.

Dictation

The nurse burst into the church.

11.4: /ɜ/   (w)or   Test Word *world*

word	worldly	worship
work	worm	worth
world	worse	

Dictation

He worked all over the world and was worth a lot of money.
The bird ate the worm.
I cannot spell that word.

11.5: /ɜ/   *ear*   Test Word *earth*

earl	earthly	learn
early	earthquake	pearl
earn	earthy	rehearse
earnest	heard	research
earth	hearse	search

Dictation

I heard he searched the earth for the pearl.
Learn your lines for the rehearsal.

11.6: /ɜ/   *our*   Test Word *journey*

journal	journey

Dictation

She wrote a journal on her journey.

11.7: /ɜ/   *olo*   Test Word *colonel*

colonel

Dictation

A colonel is an army officer.

Homophones

berth	birth
fir	fur
colonel	kernel

Dictation

What time is the ship to berth?
There were hundreds of fir trees in the woods.
The colonel had a very loud voice.

SECTION 12. /ə/　SPELLING ALTERNATIVES

1. ev**er**
2. cell**ar**
3. visit**or**
4. stat**us**
5. ac**re**
6. harb**our**
7. ridicul**ous**
8. precari**ous**
9. instantan**eous**
10. murm**ur**
11. thor**ough**
12. adequ**ate**
13. inert**ia**

12.1: /ə/　　*er*　　Test Word ev*er*

baker	higher	silver
bigger	letter	sister
braver	lower	smaller
brother	Mother	teacher
diver	never	thinner
ever	robber	wetter
father	rubber	wiser
fatter	shopper	

Dictation

My sister never writes any letters.
My father is a teacher.
I am taller and thinner than my mother.

12.2: /ə/　　*ar*　　Test Word cell*ar*

altar	collar	popular
beggar	custard	singular
burglar	grammar	vinegar
cellar	pillar	wizard

Dictation

The beggar was very popular.
The burglar hid his loot in the cellar.

12.3: /ə/　　*or*　　Test Word visit*or*
(after t,th or ss)

actor	director	professor	
author	elector	radiator	
calculator	factor	solicitor	
castor	instructor	successor	
collector	orator	tractor	visitor

Quiz

Someone who acts   = _____.
Someone who writes books = _____.
Someone who instructs   = _____.

12.4: /ə/   *us*   Test Word stat*us*

bogus	circus	minus
bonus	focus	status
census	genius	surplus
		virus

Dictation

There were surplus tickets for the circus.
He caught a virus and was very ill.
You must focus the camera before you take a picture.
He was a genius.

12.5: /ə/   *re*   Test Word ac*re*

acre	manoeuvre	ogre
calibre	massacre	sabre
centre	meagre	sceptre
fibre	mediocre	sepulchre
litre	metre	sombre
louvre	mitre	spectre
lustre	ochre	theatre

Dictation

The tree was in the centre of the acre plot.

12.6: /ə/   *our*   Test Word harb*our*

armour	harbour	parlour
behaviour	honour	rumour
colour	humour	saviour
favour	labour	vapour
flavour	neighbour	vigour
glamour	odour	

Dictation

What colour and flavour is the ice cream?
That vapour has a nasty odour.

12.7: /ə/   -ous   Test Word ridicul*ous*

adventurous	gracious	outrageous
barbarous	gorgeous	poisonous
bulbous	humorous	pompous
cautious	jealous	precious
dangerous	joyous	precipitous
delicious	marvellous	ridiculous
enormous	nervous	spacious
famous	numerous	tremendous
ferocious		

Quiz

Well known _____.
Very big   _____.
Funny   _____.

Dictation

It was very adventurous to go on that dangerous journey.
He was nervous of the poisonous gas.

12.8: /ə/   *-ious*   Test Word precar*ious*

copious	ingenious	serious
curious	insidious	tedious
devious	mysterious	various
dubious	obvious	victorious
hilarious	precarious	

Quiz

Very clever   i_____.
Strange   my_____.
Cunning   d_____.
Very funny   h_____.
Nosy   c_____.

Dictation

It was obvious that he was being serious.

12.9: /ə/   *-eous*   Test Word instantan*eous*

bounteous	extraneous	instantaneous
courteous	hideous	simultaneous
erroneous	igneous	spontaneous

Quiz

At the same time	s_____.
Very polite	c_____.
Very ugly	h_____.
On the spur of the moment	s_____.
Incorrect	e_____.
Fiery	i_____.

12.10: /ə/   *ur*   Test Word m*ur*mur

Arthur
jodhpur   murmur   Saturday

Quiz

To speak in a low voice   m_____.

Dictation

Arthur had new jodhpurs.

12.11: /ə/   *ough*   Test Word thor*ough*

thorough

Dictation

He was very thorough in his work.

12.12: /ə/   *a-e*   Test Word adequ*a*t*e*

adequate   immediate   obstinate
fortunate   intimate (Adj.)

Quiz

Stubborn	_____.	(bsaoittne)
Lucky	_____.	(oueftrnta)
At once	_____.	(meiamidet)

12.13: /ə/   *-a*   Test Word inerti*a*

dilemma   fascia   inertia
diploma   fuchsia   pagoda

Dictation

He was in a dilemma when he failed his diploma.

SECTION 13. /eɪ/   SPELLING ALTERNATIVES

1. make
2. train
3. way
4. steak
5. grey
6. straight
7. veil
8. freight
9. gaelic

13.1: /eɪ/   a-e   Test Word make

List 1

age	gate	pane
ate	hate	race
bake	Jane	rage
bale	lame	rake
cage	late	sale
cake	made	same
came	make	save
cane	male	tale
cape	mane	tame
face	mate	vale
fame	name	vane
fate	pale	wane
game		

List 2

anticipate	educate	intimate
cultivate	incubate	isolate

Dictation

Jane came to play a game.
I will bake a cake for the sale.
I hate to be late.

13.2: /eɪ/   ai   Test Word train
(Never at the end of a word)

again	gain	raise
against	maid	remain
aid	mail	sail
aim	main	snail
brain	maintain	Spain
chain	nail	stain
daisy	paid	tail
drain	pail	train
exclaim	pain	waist
explain	praise	wait
fail	rail	waive
	rain	

Dictation

I have a pain in my brain again.
Wait for the train to Spain.

13.3: /eɪ/   **ay**   **Test Word w*ay***
(At the end of a word)

always	hay	repay
away	lay	spray
bay	may	stay
day	pay	sway
dismay	play	today
gay	pray	tray
	ray	way

Dictation

I may go away to play today.
The stray dog lay in the hay all day.

13.4: /eɪ/   **ea**   **Test Word st*ea*k**

break	great	steak

Dictation

He had a great big steak in his lunch break.

13.5: /eɪ/   **ey**   **Test Word gr*ey***

convey	prey	osprey
grey	obey	

Dictation

An osprey is a bird of prey.
You must obey the rules.
She wore a grey dress.

13.6: /eɪ/   **aigh**   **Test Word str*aigh*t**

straight

Dictation

Draw a straight line.

13.7: /eɪ/   **ei**   **Test Word v*ei*l**

abseil	rein	veil
beige	reindeer	vein
feint		

Dictation

The bride wore a white veil.
Blood flows through our veins.

13.8: /eɪ/   *eigh*   Test Word fr*eigh*t

eight	inveigh	neighbour
freight	neigh	sleigh
		weight

Dictation

What weight are those eight freight containers?

13.9: /eɪ/   *ae*   Test Word *gaelic*

gaelic

Dictation

He learnt to speak gaelic.

Homophones

bail	bale	
break	brake	
faint	feint	
great	grate	
lain	lane	
maid	made	
mail	male	
main	mane	
pail	pale	
pain	pane	
plaice	place	
pray	prey	
rain	rein	reign
raise	rays	raze
sail	sale	
steak	stake	
tail	tale	
vain	vane	vein
vale	veil	
waist	waste	
ate	eight	
wait	weight	
wave	waive	

SECTION 14. /əʊ/ SPELLING ALTERNATIVES

1. note
2. boat
3. low
4. roll
5. toe
6. though
7. pianos
8. shoulder
9. yeoman
10. yolk

14.1: /əʊ/   *o-e*   Test Word note

bone	home	pope
clothe	joke	quote
code	nose	rode
coke	note	rote
cope	phone	slope
dole	poke	smoke
dome	pole	vote

Dictation

1. He left a note in code at home.
2. The pope had a red cope.

14.2: /əʊ/   *oa*   Test Word boat
(Never at the end of a word)

boast	gloat	oat
boat	goal	oath
cloak	goat	poach
coach	groan	road
coal	load	roast
coast	loaf	soak
coat	loan	soap
coax	moan	stoat
float	moat	throat
foal	oaf	toad
foam	oak	toast

Dictation

1. The toad and the goat roast toast as they float in the boat.

Quiz

How many 'oa' words can be made from the letters in the box below?

f	b	l
t	oa	s
d	c	r

14.3: /əʊ/   *ow*   **Test Word** *low*
(Usually at the end of a word)

arrow	glow	row
blow	grow	show
bow	grown	slow
bowl	know	snow
crow	low	stow
elbow	mow	
flow	own	

Note: *ew*:-sew

Dictation

1. The snow will blow low over the crow.

Quiz

1. Where your arm bends = _____.
2. A b__ and a_____.
3. Opposite of fast = _____.

14.4: /əʊ/ *o* + 2 consonants **Test Word** *roll*

bold	ghost	old
both	gold	poll
cold	hold	roll
colt	host	scold
enfold	jolt	sold
fold	most	told

Dictation

1. He sold most of his old gold.
2. She told him to hold the bolt.

Quiz

1. To be angry with someone = _____.
2. A young male horse   = _____.

14.5: /əʊ/   *oe*   **Test Word t*oe***

    doe   Joe   toe
    foe   roe   woe
    hoe

Dictation

1. Joe cut his toe with a hoe.

Quiz

1. An enemy   = _____.
2. A female deer = _____.

14.6: /əʊ/   *ough*   **Test Word th*ough***

    although   dough   though

Dictation

1. Although the dough was moist, the bread was dry.

14.7: /əʊ/   *o*   **Test Word pianos**

    dynamo   maestro   radio
    go   no   so
    hero   piano   solo
    limbo   polo   tomato
    lo   potato

Dictation

1. Do not go so far.
2. The hero ate a tomato and a potato and then played polo.

14.8: /əʊ/   *ou*   **Test Word sho*u*lder**

boulder	moult	shoulder
mouldy	mould	soul

Dictation

1. The poor soul put a mouldy boulder on his shoulder.

14.9: /əʊ/   *eo*   **Test Word y*eo*man**

yeoman

Quiz

Another name for a Beefeater = _____ of the guard.

14.10: /əʊ/   *ol*

folk	yolk

Homophones

groan	grown	
loan	lone	
road	rode	rowed
roll	role	
sew	sow	so
soul	sole	
thrown	throne	
yoke	yolk	

SECTION 15. /aɪ/   SPELLING ALTERNATIVES

1. p**i**p**e**
2. fl**y**
3. f**igh**t
4. f**i**nd
5. p**ie**
6. d**ye**
7. b**uy**
8. **ei**ther
9. d**ia**l
10. m**ae**stro

15.1: /aɪ/   *i-e*   **Test Word k*i*t*e***

bike	line	side
bite	mile	slide
dine	mine	slime
file	Nile	smile
fine	nine	spine
hide	pine	time
ice	pipe	vile
jive	quite	vine
kite	rice	wide
like	ride	wine
lime	ripe	

Dictation

1. I like to ride my bike.
2. That kite is mine.

Quiz

How many i-e words can be made from the letters in the box below?

_____

s   m   t

_____

k   i-e   p

_____

r   l   d

_____

15.2: /aɪ/   *y*   **Test Word fl*y***

asylum	hydrant	rhyme
bicycle	hygiene	satisfy
by	hydra	shy
cry	July	sky
cyclone	multiply	sly
cypress	my	spy
dry	nylon	style
dynamic	pry	try
dynamite	psychic	thyme
fly	pylon	type
fry	python	typhoid
guy	rely	why
gyro	reply	xylophone

Dictation

1. Try not to be shy or cry.   2. I will fly in the sky in July.

15.3: /aɪ/   *igh*   **Test Word flight**

bright	light	sigh
fight	might	sight
flight	mighty	thigh
fright	night	tight
high	plight	
knight	right	

Note: *eigh*   height

Dictation

1. The knight might fight tonight.
2. The bright light gave him a fright.

Quiz

1. It is dark, put on the _____.
2. We go to sleep at _____.
3. The ghost gave him a _____.
4. Well done, you got that sum _____.
5. The opposite of low = _____.
6. The opposite of loose = _____.
7. Glasses improve your eye_____.

15.4: /aɪ/ *i + 2 consonants*   **Test Word find**

behind	grind	pint
bind	hind	rind
blind	kind	wild
child	mild	wind
find	mind	

Dictation

1. The child was kind to the blind man.

15.5: /aɪ/   *ie*   **Test Word pie**

die	lie	tie
fie	pie	

Make 4 words from the letters and use them in sentences.

_____

l
_____

d   ie   t
_____

p
_____

15.6: /aɪ/   *ye*   **Test Word d*ye***

bye   dye   rye

Note: eye

Dictation

1. She got dye in her eye.

15.7: /aɪ/   *uy*   **Test Word b*uy***

buy

Dictation

1. She went to buy a dress.

15.8: /aɪ/   *ei*   **Test Word *ei*ther**

eiderdown   either   neither
Eiffel Tower

Dictation

1. Have either of you got an eiderdown?

15.9: /aɪ/   *ia*   **Test Word d*ia*l**

dial

Dictation

1. Will you dial the number for me?

15.10: /aɪ/   *ae*   **Test Word m*ae*stro**

maestro   minutiae

Dictation

1. The orchestra thought the conductor was a maestro.

Homophones

aisle	isle	I'll
buy	by	bye
die	dye	
find	fined	
knight	night	
might	mite	
right	rite	
sight	site	
stile	style	
thyme	time	
tide	tied	

SECTION 16. /aʊ/   SPELLING ALTERNATIVES

1. clown
2. house
3. plough

16.1: /aʊ/   *ow*   Test Word clown

bow	fowl	now
clown	gown	sow
cow	growl	towel
crowd	how	town
crown	howl	vow
down	now	vowel
drown	powder	

Dictation

1. The crowd threw flowers at the clown.
2. On the farm there were sows, cows and fowl.

Quiz

1. Every syllable must have a _____.
2. Dry yourself with a _____.

16.2: /aʊ/   *ou*   Test Word house
(Never at the end of a word)

bound	house	pound
bout	loud	round
cloud	louse	scout
count	mound	sound
foul	mount	stout
found	mouth	trout
ground	noun	wound
hound	out	

Dictation

1. We found a house with big grounds.
2. That scout has a loud mouth.

16.3: /aʊ/   *ough*   **Test Word pl*ough***

     bough   plough   Slough

Dictation

1. He got the plough in Slough.

Quiz

Part of a tree = _____.

               Homophones

           aloud   allowed
           bough   bow
           foul   fowl

Dictation

1. I am not allowed to read aloud.

SECTION 17. /ɔɪ/   SPELLING ALTERNATIVES

             1. boy
             2. coin

17.1: /ɔɪ/   *oy*   **Test Word b*oy***

     annoy   employ   Roy
     boy   enjoy   royal
     convoy   joy   toy
     coy   loyal   voyage
     destroy   oyster

Dictation

1. Roy is a coy boy.
2. It will annoy him if you destroy his toys.
3. The loyal royal prince ate oysters on the voyage.

17.2: /ɔɪ/   *oi*   **Test Word *coin***
(never at the end of a word)

avoid	foil	poise
boil	hoist	poison
choice	join	soil
coil	joint	spoil
coin	noise	toil
disappoint	oil	toilet
disjoint	point	voice
exploit		

Dictation

1. Avoid eating poison!
2. That noise will spoil your voice.

Homophones

boy   buoy

Dictation

1. The boy swam to the buoy.

SECTION 18. /ɪə/   SPELLING ALTERNATIVES

1. f**ear**
2. d**eer**
3. m**ere**
4. w**eir**d
5. p**ier**
6. th**eor**y
7. **ey**rie

18.1: /ɪə/   *ear*   **Test Word *fear***

appear	ear	near
clear	fear	spear
dear	gear	year
disappear	hear	

Dictation

1. I can hear you clearly when you speak near my ear.

18.2: /ɪə/   *eer*   **Test Word *deer***

career	engineer	steer
cheer	jeer	veer
deer	peer	
eerie	queer	

Dictation

1. The children cheered when they saw the deer.
2. He had a good career as an engineer.

18.3: /ɪə/ *er* + vowel   Test Word m*ere*

experience	mere	sphere
here	period	zero
interfere	severe	

Dictation

1. The world is a sphere.
2. Here comes the severe teacher.

18.4: /ɪə/   *eir*   Test Word w*eir*d

Madeira	weir	weird

Dictation

1. We saw a weird weir in Madeira.

18.5: /ɪə/   *ier*   Test Word p*ier*

brigadier	pier	tier
fierce	pierce	

Dictation

1. The fierce brigadier had his ears pierced on the pier.
2. The wedding cake has three tiers.

18.6: /ɪə/   *eor*   Test Word th*eory*

theorem	theory

Dictation

1. He had to learn theory of music.

18.7: /ɪə/   *eyr*   Test Word *eyr*ie

eyrie

Dictation

1. An eagle's home is called an eyrie.

Homophones

cereal	serial
dear	deer
eyrie	eerie
hear	here
pier	peer
tier	tear

SECTION 19. /ɛə/   SPELLING ALTERNATIVES

1. wh**ere**		5. b**ear**
2. ch**air**		6. m**ayor**
3. th**eir**		7. pr**ayer**
4. r**are**		8. **aer**oplane

19.1: /ɛə/   *ere*   Test Word wh*ere*

there	where

Dictation

1. "Where is your coat?"
2. "It's over there."

19.2: /ɛə/   *air*   Test Word ch*air*

air	fair	pair
chair	hair	stair
chairman	lair	

Dictation

1. The girl with fair hair sat on the chair.
2. The chairman walked up the stairs.

19.3: /ɛə/   *eir*   Test Word th*eir*

heir	heirloom
heiress	their

Dictation

1. The heir will inherit a valuable heirloom.

19.4: /ɛə/   *are*   Test Word r*are*

bare	hare	share
care	mare	spare
dare	pare	stare
fare	rare	wares

Dictation

1. That is a rare hare.

Quiz

1. I must pay my bus ____.
2. I have got a ____ tyre.
3. Female horse = ____.
4. Look closely = _____.

19.5: /ɛə/   *ear*   **Test Word b*ear***

  bear   pear   swear
  wear

Dictation

1. I swear that bear was eating a pear.

19.6: /ɛə/   *ayor*   **Test Word m*ayor***

  mayor

Dictation

1. He went to the Lord Mayor's show.

19.7: /ɛə/   *ayer*   **Test Word pr*ayer***

  layer   prayer

Dictation

1. He said a prayer.

19.8: /ɛə/   *aer*   **Test Word *aer*oplane**

  aerate   aerodrome   aerosol
  aerial   aerodynamics
  aerobatics   aeroplane

Dictation

1. The aeroplane did aerobatics over the aerodrome.

Homophones

air	heir	
bare	bear	
fare	fair	
hare	hair	
mare	mayor	
pare	pair	pear
stare	stair	
their	there	

SECTION 20. /ʊə/   SPELLING ALTERNATIVES

1. poor
2. sure
3. tour

20.1: /ʊə/   *oor*   Test Word p*oor*

boor	moor	poor

Dictation

1. The poor man walked on the moor.

20.2: /ʊə/   *ure*   Test Word s*ure*

allure	sure

20.3: /ʊə/   *our*   Test Word t*our*

dour	tour

Dictation

1. The dour man went on a tour of the city.

SECTION 21. /ju/   SPELLING ALTERNATIVES

1. cube
2. few
3. music
4. queue
5. neutral
6. beautiful

21.1: /ju/   *u-e*   Test Word c*u*b*e*

altitude	due	tube
amuse	excuse	tune
cube	fuse	use
cute	mute	

Dictation

1. Use a fuse in the plug.
2. A cube and a tube are shapes.

Quiz

Silent   = _____.
Very sweet = _____.

21.2: /ju/   *ew*   **Test Word *few***

dew	knew	stew
few	new	
jew	pew	

Note: ewe

Dictation

1. He sat on the new pew.
2. We knew there was dew on the grass.

21.3: /ju/   *u-V*   **Test Word music**

amusing	music
funeral	puny
	tunic

Dictation

1. He amused her by playing music.
2. The romans wore tunics.

21.4: /ju/   *eue*   **Test Word qu*eue***

queue

21.5: /ju/   *eu*   **Test Word n*eu*tral**

deuce	feud	neutron
deuteronomy	feudal	pneumatic
euphorium	leukaemia	pseudo
euphoria	neutral	rheumatism
euphoric	neutralise	Teutonic

21.6: /ju/   *eau*

beautiful

SECTION 22. /juə/   SPELLING ALTERNATIVES

1. pure

22.1: /juə/   *ure*   Test Word p*ure*

cure	endure	manure
demure	impure	mature
		pure

Dictation

1. This pure drink will cure you.

SECTION 23. /aɪə/   SPELLING ALTERNATIVES

1. **f**i**re**
2. **d**i**a**ry
3. **l**yre
4. ch**oir**
5. **fie**ry
6. v**io**lent

23.1: /aɪə/   *ire*   Test Word f*ire*

dire	mire	umpire
fire	sire	wire
hire	tire	

Dictation

1. It would be dire if the wire caught fire.
2. We had to hire an umpire for the match.

23.2: /aɪə/   *ia*   Test Word d*ia*ry

bias	briar	dialogue
diary		

Dictation

1. She recorded their dialogue in her diary.

23.3: /aɪə/   *yr*   Test Word l*yre*

gyrate	lyre	pyre

Quiz

1. Stringed musical instrument = _____.
2. To revolve   = _____.

23.4: /aɪə/   *oir*   **Test Word ch*oir***

choir

Dictation

1. She sang in the school choir.

23.5: /aɪə/   *ier*   **Test Word *fiery***

fiery

Dictation

1. He had a fiery temper.

23.6: /aɪə/   *io*   **Test Word v*io*lent**

violate   violent   violet

Dictation

1. He was a violent criminal

SECTION 24. /ɑʊə/   SPELLING ALTERNATIVES

1. h**our**
2. p**ower**

24.1: /ɑʊə/   *our*   **Test Word h*our***

flour   our   sour
hour

Dictation

1. Our flour tastes sour.

24.2: /ɑʊə/   *ower*   **Test Word p*ower***

bower   glower   tower
cower   power
flower   shower

Quiz

Make "ower" words from the letters below and use them in sentences.

l	s	h

l	ower	b

c	t	g

Homophones

flower flour
hour   our

CONSONANTS

PLOSIVES

1. /p/
2. /b/
3. /t/
4. /d/
5. /k/
6. /g/
7. /kw/

SECTION 1. /p/   SPELLING ALTERNATIVES

1. **p**in
2. ha**pp**y

1.1: /p/   *p*   Test Word *p*ig
(pp in the middle of a
word after a short vowel)

Initial		Final		pp
pack	pin	cap	rope	capped
pain	pine	cup	scope	dripped
pan	pink	damp	scrap	happy
pea	plug	drop	shop	kipper
pen	plum	hip	sip	mapped
pet	poke	hop	snip	nappy
Pete	pole	hope	stamp	puppy
pick	poor	jump	tip	quipped
pie	pot	map	trap	ripped
pig	pram	rip	trip	shopping
pill	pull	ripe	type	stopper
	put			topping
				whipped

Dictation

1. Put the pet pig in the pram.
2. Drop the plums in the pan.

SECTION 2. /b/   SPELLING ALTERNATIVES

1. **b**it
2. ca**bb**age

2.1: /b/   *b*   **Test Word *boat***

(bb in the middle of a
word after a short vowel)

Initial		Final		bb
baby	bit	Bob	mob	bobbing
bat	black	cab	rib	cabbage
beat	bane	dub	rob	ebbed
bell	boot	dab	snob	fibber
bet	bright	fib	sob	grabbing
big	buzz	job	web	hobby
bin		knob		mobbed
				rabbit
				stabbing
				webbed

Exercise

Add b to these words and then use them in sentences.

ell, ru, we_, _a_y, _et.

SECTION 3. /t/   SPELLING ALTERNATIVES

1. **t**en
2. ma**tt**
3. **Th**ames
4. dou**b**t
5. recei**p**t
6. indi**ct**

3.1: /t/   *t*   **Test Word *ten***

(tt in the middle of a
word after a short vowel)

Initial		Final		tt
tail	tight	bet	hit	button
tame	time	boot	met	cutter
tap	to	cat	put	fatter
team	toad	fat	shot	getting
tell	top	flat	sit	hotter
ten	tug	hat	spot	kitten
			yet	letter
				mutton
				putting
				quitter
				rotten
				setting
				totter
				wetter

Dictation

1. Ten tame toads sat on top of the tap.

3.2: /t/   **Final *tt* Test Word ma*tt***

     butt   matt   putt   sett   watt

Dictation

1. A badger lives in a sett.
2. Would you like matt or gloss paint?

3.3: /t/   *th*   **Test Word *Th*ames**

     Esther   Thailand   Thames   Thomas   thyme

Dictation

1. Thomas grows thyme near the Thames.

3.4: /t/   *bt*   **Test Word dou*bt***

     debt   doubt   subtle

Dictation

1. I doubt if I can pay my debt.

3.5: /t/   *pt*   **Test Word recei*pt***

     receipt

Dictation

1. Please may I have a receipt?

3.6: /t/   *ct*   **Test Word indi*ct***

     indict

Anagram

ndicit = accuse

SECTION 4. /d/   SPELLING ALTERNATIVES

1. **d**o
2. a**dd**

4.1: /d/   *d*   **Test Word** *d*o
(dd in the middle of a
word after a short vowel)

Initial		Final		pp
did	down	bed	mad	baddy
dig	duck	bid	mind	Daddy
din	duke	Dad	mud	giddy
do	dug	head	pad	hidden
dot		hid	said	kidding
		hide	wed	madden
		kind		paddock
				ridden
				sudden
				teddy
				wedding

Dictation

1. Did the big duck dig in the mud?

4.2: /d/   *dd*   **Test Word** a*dd*

add   odd

Dictation

1. Add the odd numbers.

SECTION 5. /k/   SPELLING ALTERNATIVES

1. **c**lap
2. **k**ite
3. bla**ck**
4. magi**c**
5. a**ch**e
6. grotes**que**
7. a**cc**ount
8. **qu**ay

5.1: /k/   *c*   **Test Word *clap***

Write c before a, o, u or any consonant.

ca		*co*	*cu*	*c +* *consonant*
cab	card	coal	cub	act
cage	care	coat	cube	clan
cake	carpet	cod	cup	clap
calf	carry	coin	cut	clip
call	case	cold	cute	cling
camp	cash	cook		cloth
can	cat	cost		cloud
cap	catch	cot		cream
car	cave	count		crest
		cover		crew
				cricket
				crime
				crisp
				crow
				cry
				pact

Dictation

1. The cook cut the cake.
2. Can you call the cat?

Quiz

Opposite of hot = _____.
Weep   = _____.
A young fox   = _____.

5.2: /k/   *k*   **Test Word *kite***

Write k before e, i or y or at the end of a word, after a consonant or a long vowel.

ke	**ki**	**ky**	**k**	
broke	kid	hanky	ask	rook
keen	kill	lanky	bank	sank
keep	kind		book	sink
Ken	king		chalk	talk
kennel	kipper		drink	tank
Kent	kiss		ink	think
key	kit		look	trunk
lake	kite		pink	whisk
wake	kitten			

Dictation

1. The kind king gave the kid his key.

5.3: /k/   *ck*   **Test Word bla*ck***

After /æ/ /ɛ/ /ɪ/ /ɒ/ and /ʌ/ (short vowels) write ck.

/æ/	/ɛ/	/ɪ/	/ɒ/	/ʌ/
back	beck	chick	block	cluck
black	deck	crick	clock	duck
crack	fleck	flick	dock	luck
knack	neck	kick	flock	muck
lack	peck	lick	lock	suck
pack	speck	pick	rock	stuck
quack	wreck	prick	shock	truck
rack		sick	sock	
sack		stick		
smack		thick		
snack				
tack				
track				

Dictation

1. Pack the clock in the sack.
2. I was sick with shock.
3. The hen went cluck and the duck went quack.

5.4: /k/   *ic*   **Test Word mag*ic***

Words of more than one syllable ending with /k/ write ic.

arithmetic	domestic	fantastic	magnetic	scientific
artistic	economic	frantic	panic	terrific
athletic	elastic	heroic	picnic	tonic
Atlantic	electric	historic	plastic	topic
comic	energetic	magic	public	traffic

Dictation

1. The solo flight across the Atlantic was heroic.
2. The traffic was horrific and the public was frantic.

Quiz

1. An outdoor meal = _____.
2. Number work = _____.
3. Stretchy material = _____.
4. Good at art = _____.

5.5: /k/   *ch*   Test Word a*ch*e

ache	character	Christine	mechanic	school
anchor	chemist	Christmas	orchestra	stomach
architect	choir	Christopher	scheme	technical
architecture	chorus	Chronicle	schizoid	technique
chaos	Christ	echo	schizoph-renia	

Dictation

1. Christopher got a chemistry set for Christmas.
2. The school orchestra gives me a headache.
3. The chemist cured Christine's stomach ache.

5.6: /k/   *que*   Test Word grotes*que*

antique	grotesque	picturesque	technique	unique
cheque	oblique			

Dictation

1. The man paid by cheque for the unique antique.

5.7: /k/   *cc*   Test Word a*cc*ount

acclaim	accord	accuse	occupation	recce
accolade	accost	buccaneer	occupy	succour
accommodate	account	occasion	occur	succulent
accompany	accumulate	occult	raccoon	succumb
accomplice	accurate			

Dictation

1. His occupation was accountancy.
2. He was accused of occupying the wrong accommodation.

5.8: /k/   *qu*   Test Word *qu*ay

conquer	quay	quiche	quorum	tequila
liquor	queue	quoit		

Note: la**cqu**er

Dictation

1. He ate quiche and drank liquor on the quay.

SECTION 6. /g/   SPELLING ALTERNATIVES

1. mug   3. **g**uilty
2. e**gg**   4. **gh**ost

6.1: /g/   g   Test Word mug
(gg in the middle of a
word after a short vowel)

g is usually followed by o, a, u or any consonant.

ga	go	gu	g + consonant	final	gg
gag	go	gull	glad	bag	baggage
gain	goal	gulf	glass	dog	tagging
gale	goat	gulp	glide	fog	jogger
gallon	god	gum	globe	hug	lugged
gallop	gold	gun	glove	jig	muggy
game	golf	gush	glow	mug	nugget
gang	gone	gust	grab	peg	ragged
gas	good	gut	grand	rug	soggy
gate	got	gutter	grasp	stag	wagging
			green		

Note g followed by e or i.

ge	gi
gear	gibbon
get	giddy
gelding	gift
	giggle
	gill
	gilt
	girl
	give

6.2: /g/   Final   gg   Test Word egg

egg

6.3: /g/   gu   Test Word guilty

Write u after g when the next letter is e, i or y, to keep the hard /**g**/ sound.

guess	guidance	guy	catalogue
guest	guide		colleague
guerilla	guild		dialogue
Guernsey	guile		fatigue
	guillotine		fugue
	guilt		league
	guilty		plague
	guinea		rogue
	guitar		tongue
			vague
			vogue

Note: guard guardian guarantee

Dictation

1. Guess who was my guest in Guernsey.
2. Guy played the guitar.
3. The prologue was very vague.

6.4: /g/   *gh*   Test Word *ghost*

aghast	ghastly	ghostly
dinghy	ghost	ghoul

Dictation

1. We saw a ghastly ghost in the dinghy.

SECTION 7. /kw/   SPELLING ALTERNATIVES

1. **qu**it
2. **ch**oir
3. a**cqu**ire

7.1: /kw/   *qu*   Test Word *quit*
q is always followed by u

quack	queer	quilt	conquest	squash
quad	quest	quip	inquire	squat
quake	question	quite	request	squeak
quaint	quick	quiver	require	squeal
quality	quid	quota	squalid	squire
quarrel	quiet	quote	square	squirm
queen	quill			

Dictation

1. The quarrel with the queen made him quake and quiver.
2. A mouse squeaks and a duck quacks.

7.2: /kw/   *ch*   Test Word *choir*

choir

Dictation

1. She sings in a choir.

7.3: /kw/   *cqu*   Test Word *acquire*

acquaint   acquaintance   acquire   acquit   acquitted

Dictation

1. The suspect was acquitted.

NASALS

8. /m/
9. /n/ (n)
10. /ŋ/
11. /ŋg/

SECTION 8. /m/   SPELLING ALTERNATIVES

1. **m**ake
2. cli**mb**
3. autu**mn**

8.1: /m/   *m*   **Test Word *m*ake**
(mm in the middle of a
word after a short vowel)

Initial		Final		mm
mad	milk	calm	him	dummy
made	mind	come	jam	humming
man	mood	from	rum	jammed
map	mouse	gum	sum	Mummy
may	move	harm	Tom	rimmed
me	must			simmer
meet	my			skimmed
met				

Dictation

1. My mum made me swim with Tom.

8.2: /m/   *mb*   **Test Word cli*mb***

bomb	dumb	numb	succumb	tomb
climb	lamb	plumber	thumb	womb
comb	limb			

Dictation

1. The plumber climbed up the pipe.
2. My thumb has gone numb.

8.3: /m/   *mn*   **Test Word autu*mn***

autumn	condemn	damn	hymn	solemn
column				

Dictation

1. We sang a solemn hymn about autumn.

SECTION 9. /n/ /ŋ/   SPELLING ALTERNATIVES

1. **n**ote
2. happ**en**
3. drag**on**
4. org**an**
5. **kn**ife
6. barga**in**
7. mod**ern**
8. **gn**aw
9. **pn**eumonia
10. **mn**emonic

9.1: /n/   *n*   Test Word *n*ote
(nn in the middle of a
word after a short vowel)

Initial		Final		nn
name	nit	bin	run	banned
nap	no	fin	sun	canning
neat	nose	gun	ten	dinner
net	not	hen	van	fanned
nine	note	men	win	gunned
nip	nut	pin		pinned
				running
				sunny
				tanned

Dictation

1. Nine men ran for fun in the sun.

9.2: /n/   *en*   Test Word happ*en*

bitten	eaten	happen	shaken	wooden
broken	given	hidden	stolen	woollen
chosen	golden	rotten	taken	

Dictation

1. The dozen hidden golden rings were stolen.

9.3: /n/   *on*   Test Word drag*on*

apron	button	dragon	lemon	mutton
bacon	cotton			

Dictation

1. I need cotton to put a button on the apron.

9.4: /n/   **an**   **Test Word organ**

human   organ   orphan   sultan   woman

Dictation

1. The woman played the organ to the sultan.

9.5: /n/   **kn**   **Test Word knife**

knapsack	kneel	knit	knock	know
knave	knew	knitting	knoll	knowledge
knead	knickers	knob	knot	knuckle
knee	knife			
	knight			

Dictation

1. Knock on the door with your knuckles.
2. I know a knight who knits knickers on his knees.

9.6: /n/   **ain**   **Test Word bargain**

bargain	curtain	mountain	porcelain	villain
certain	fountain			

Dictation

1. The villain was certain the curtain was a bargain.

9.7: /n/   **ern**   **Test Word modern**

cavern   eastern   govern   modern   tavern

Dictation

1. They turned the cavern into a modern tavern.

9.8: /n/   **gn**   **Test Word gnaw**

gnarl	gnaw	align	benign	malign
gnash	gnome	assign	consign	resign
gnat	gnu	assignment	design	sign

Dictation

1. The gnu gnashed his teeth at the gnome.

9.9: /n/   **pn**   **Test Word pneumonia**

pneumatic   pneumonia

Dictation

1. He caught pneumonia using a pneumatic drill.

9.10: /n/   ***mn***   **Test Word *mnemonic***

mnemonic

Dictation

1. A mnemonic is a memory aid.

SECTION 10. /ŋ/   SPELLING ALTERNATIVES

1. bri**ng**
2. ba**nk**
3. ton**gue**

10.1: /ŋ/   ***ng***   **Test Word bri*ng***

among	fling	long	spring	thing
bang	hang	ring	sting	wing
bring	hung	sing	string	young
cling	king	song		

Dictation

1. The young king sang a long song.

10.2: /ŋ/   ***n (k)***   **Test Word ba*nk***

bank	ink	pink	shrink	think
blank	junk	rink	stink	trunk
drink	link	sank	tank	wink
drunk				

Dictation

1. The pink ink is in the trunk.

10.3: /ŋ/   ***gue***   **Test Word ton*gue***

harangue   meringue   tongue

Dictation

1. Lick the meringue with your tongue.

SECTION 11. /ŋg/   SPELLING ALTERNATIVES

1. **finger**

11.1: /ŋg/   *ng*   **Test Word fi*ng*er**

anger	dangle	jingle	mangle	strangle
angle	finger	jungle	mingle	tangle
bangle	hunger	linger	single	tingle

Dictation

1. She cried when her bangle fell in the mangle.

FRICATIVES

12. /f/
13. /v/
14. /θ/
15. /ð/
16. /s/
17. /z/
18. /ʃ/
19. /ʒ/
20. /h/

SECTION 12. /f/   SPELLING ALTERNATIVES

1. **f**eet
2. sni**ff**
3. **ph**one
4. cou**gh**

12.1: /f/   *f*   **Test Word *feet***

Initial			Final	
fan	first		calf	proof
fat	fist		half	reef
feast	fire		knife	safe
feet	fog		leaf	thief
fin	foot		life	
fine	fun			

Dictation

1. Fish have fins.
2. Fred is five feet tall.

12.2: /f/   *ff*   **Test Word sni*ff***

After /ɑ/ /ɪ/ /ɒ/ and /ʌ/ write ff.

/ɑ/	/ɪ/	/ɒ/	/ʌ/
staff	cliff	off	bluff
	sniff	offer	cuff
	stiff		fluff
			gruff
			huff
			puff
			snuff
			stuff

Dictation

1. The gruff man fell off the cliff.
2. Have a sniff of this snuff.

12.3: /f/   *ph*   **Test Word *ph*one**

alphabet	hyphen	phantom	phony	prophet
elephant	megaphone	phase	phosphate	symphony
emphasis	microphone	pheasant	photograph	telegraph
geography	nephew	Philip	physical	telephone
graph	orphan	phoneme	physician	triumph
graphics	paragraph	phonic	physics	

Note: **pph**   sapphire

Dictation

1. My nephew took a photograph of the elephant.
2. The opening phrase of the symphony was a triumph for the composer.
3. The physician emphasised the importance of physical exercise.

12.4: /f/   *gh*   **Test Word cou*gh***

cough	enough	rough	tough	trough
draught	laugh			

Dictation

1. I get a rough cough from sitting in the draught.

SECTION 13. /v/   SPELLING ALTERNATIVES

1. have

13.1: /v/   *v*   **Test Word *have***

There is always an e after final v.

vain	vest	above	leave
vale	vet	active	live
van	vice	drive	move
vast	vine	five	save
veal	vole	glove	shave
very	volt	grove	shove
		have	slave

Dictation

1. The vet drove his van very fast.

SECTION 14. /θ/   SPELLING ALTERNATIVES

1. **th**ink

14.1: /θ/   *th*   **Test Word *th*ink**

	Initial			Final	
thank	thirsty	three	bath	North
thick	thirteen	threw	both	path
thief	thirty	through	month	tenth
thin	thorn	throw	mouth	
think	thought	thumb		
third				

Dictation

1. The thin thief had a thick thorn in his thumb.

SECTION 15. /ð/   SPELLING ALTERNATIVES

1. **th**en

15.1: /ð/   *th*   **Test Word *th*en**

	Initial		Final	
than	there	although	mother
that	they	another	other
the	this	bother	weather
their	those	brother	whether
them	though		
then			

Dictation

1. The man over there is my father's brother.

SECTION 16. /s/   SPELLING ALTERNATIVES

1. **s**ad   5. li**s**ten
2. dre**ss**   6. **s**word
3. hou**se**   7. **s**cience
4. **c**ycle   8. **p**salm

16.1: /s/   s   Test Word *s*ad

Initial

			Final	
sack	seat	soft	bus	thus
sad	see	song	gas	us
sap	set	smoke	this	yes
say	sit	snow		

Dictation

1. Sid sat on the seat and sang a sad song.
2. Mum met us at the bus.

16.2: /s/   *ss*   Test Word dre*ss*

After /ɑ/ /æ/ /ɛ/ /ɪ/ /ɒ/ and /ʌ/ write ss

/ɑ/	/æ/	/ɛ/	/ɪ/	/ɒ/
class	ass	dress	hiss	boss
glass	lass	guess	kiss	cross
grass	mass	mess	miss	floss
		press	Swiss	gloss
				moss

/ʌ/
fuss

Note: /əʊ/ + ss - gross
Note: bus, gas, us, this and yes.

Dictation

1. My cross boss made a fuss.
2. Bess must press her dress.

16.3: /s/   *se*   Test Word hou*se*

Final s is followed by e.

cease	decease	house	loose	release
coarse	dense	immense	mouse	rinse
course	goose	increase	practise	sense
			(verb)	tense

Dictation

1. The mouse was loose in the house.
2. Of course I will release the goose.

16.4: /s/   c   Test Words *cycle device*

C followed by e, i or y makes the /s/ sound. (Soft c.)

ce		ci	cy
ace	mice	accident	cyclamen
advice	nice	circle	cycle
cell	parcel	circus	cyclone
cellar	pence	citizen	cygnet
centre	place	city	cylinder
certain	police	civil	cymbal
concert	practice (noun)	decide	cynical
dance	price	excite	Cypress
December	race	pencil	juicy
device	recent	racing	Lucy
except	space		Percy
face			

Dictation

1. I notice there is a nice concert on in December.
2. We decided to go to the circus in the centre of the city.
3. Lucy cycled to see the cygnets in the park.
4. I advise you to take that device away.
5. I followed his advice and practised every day.

Quiz

1. Larger than a town = ____.
2. A prison room = ____.
3. More than one mouse = ____.
4. The twelfth month = _____.
5. A baby swan = _____.

16.5: /s/   st   Test Word li**st**en

bristle	castle	hasten	jostle	thistle
bustle	glisten	hustle	listen	trestle
				whistle

Dictation

1. Listen for the whistle then hasten to the castle.

16.6: /s/   sw   Test Word *sword*

answer   sword

Quiz

1. The opposite of question = _____.
2. A weapon = _____.

16.7: /s/　　　　　　*sc*　　　　**Test Word *science***

ascend	scenery	sciatica	scientist	scissors
descend	sceptre	science	scintillate	scythe
scene	scent	scientific		

Dictation

1. The scientist discovered a new scent.
2. On the ascent we saw the lovely scenery.

16.8: /s/　　　　　　*ps*　　　　**Test Word *psalm***

psalm	psychic	psychology
pseudo	psychiatry	

Dictation

1. The psychologist sang psalms in church.

SECTION 17. /z/　　　　SPELLING ALTERNATIVES

1. **z**oo
2. shoe**s**
3. po**ss**ess
4. choo**s**e
5. **x**erox

17.1: /z/　　　　　　*z*　　　　**Test Word *zoo***

Initial			Final	
zany	zip		amaze	quiz
zeal	zither		blaze	seize
zebra	zodiac		crazy	authorize
zen	zone		graze	baptize
zero	zoo		lazy	familiarize
zinc	zoom		maze	sterilize
zigzag	zulu		prize	symbolize

Note: buzz, fizz, fuzz, jazz, whizz

Dictation

1. The lazy zebra was in the zoo.

17.2: /z/   s   Test Word shoes

Final 's' after a voiced consonant or vowel.

boys	dogs	mends	plays	sings
cars	keys	monkeys	radios	tables
cools	laws	obeys	shoes	toys
days	leaves	pigs		

Dictation

1. The men's keys are in the cars.
2. My husband's cousin is a miser.

17.3: /z/   ss   Test Word possess

dessert	dissolve	hussar	possess	scissors

Dictation

1. The hussar ate too much dessert.
2. I possess two pairs of scissors.

17.4: /z/   s   Test Words advise
choose

advise	choose	ease	phase	raisin
arouse	cousin	husband	phrase	revise
baptism	devise	miser	please	surprise
bruise	disease			

Dictation

1. Please choose some food.

17.5: /z/   x   Test Word xerox

xerox	xylophone

Dictation

1. She learnt to play the xylophone.

SECTION 18. /ʃ/   SPELLING ALTERNATIVES

1. shed   6. mission
2. sure   7. pension
3. operation   8. brochure
4. partial   9. ocean
5. ancient   10. conscious

18.1: /ʃ/   *sh*   **Test Word *shed***

Initial			Final	
shake	sheep	shock	bush	dish
shall	sheet	shoe	blush	fish
shark	shine	shoot	cash	rush
she	ship	shop	crash	splash
shed	shirt	show	crush	wash
shell			dash	wish

Dictation

1. She shall get the shell.
2. She showed me the shirt shop.
3. A shark is a fish.

18.2: /ʃ/   *s + ss*   **Test Word *sure***

assure	reassure	sugar	sure	surely

Dictation

1. Are you sure you want sugar?
2. He assured me he was reassured by the good news.

18.3: /ʃ/   *ti* (on)   **Test Word *operation***

absorption	elation	notion
action	election	observation
addition	examination	perfection
attention	fraction	population
collection	frustration	portion
commotion	function	position
competition	information	potion
completion	inscription	pollution
composition	institution	preposition
connection	inspection	protection
corporation	intention	recognition
decoration	invention	reflection
depletion	junction	repetition
devotion	lotion	section
dictionary	mention	selection
direction	motion	solution
edition	nation	station
education		

Dictation

1. We met our relations at the station.
2. I wrote a composition about the election for my examination.
3. A dictionary gives useful information.
4. The nations population is growing.

18.4: /ʃ/   ti   Test Word par*ti*al

circumstantial	inertia	partial
confidential	influential	patient
essential	initial	torrential

Dictation

1. This letter is confidential.
2. It is essential that I am on time.
3. Write your initials here.
4. You must learn to be patient.

18.5: /ʃ/   ci   Test Word an*ci*ent

ancient	gracious	politician	special	sufficient
delicious	musician	precious	species	suspicion
especially	official	social		

Dictation

1. We had a special meal, it was delicious.
2. The musician's violin is very precious.

18.6: /ʃ/   ssi   Test Word mi*ssi*on

admission	expression	passion	profession	succession
aggression	impression	permission	Russia	suppression
compassion	mission	possession	session	transmission
discussion	oppression	procession		

Note: issue, pressure, tissue

Dictation

1. We had a discussion about the medical profession.
2. What was your impression of Russia?

18.7: /ʃ/   consonant + si   Test Word pension

A consonant followed by si makes the /ʃ/ sound.

aversion	diversion	mansion	pension	version
comprehension				

Dictation

1. He had an aversion to doing comprehensions.
2. We followed the diversion signs.

18.8: /ʃ/   ch   Test Word bro*ch*ure

brochure	champagne	chauffeur	chivalry	machinery
chalet	chateau	chef	machine	parachute

Dictation

1. Put the clothes in the washing machine.
2. The chef and the chauffeur worked in the chateau.
3. They celebrated with a bottle of champagne.

18.9: /ʃ/   *ce*   **Test Word o*ce*an**

herbaceous   ocean

Dictation

1. The plants grew in the herbaceous border.
2. He sailed across the Atlantic ocean.

18.10: /ʃ/   *sci*   **Test Word con*sci*ous**

conscious   luscious   unconscious

Dictation

1. He was unconscious after the accident.

SECTION 19. /ʒ/   SPELLING ALTERNATIVES

1. televi**si**on   3. presti**ge**
2. mea**su**re   4. sei**z**ure

19.1: /ʒ/   *si*   **Test Word televi*si*on**

A vowel followed by si makes the /ʒ/ sound.

collision	decision	explosion	intrusion	precision
collusion	delusion	fusion	invasion	provision
conclusion	erosion	inclusion	occasion	revision
confusion	exclusion			

Dictation

1. There was confusion when we heard an explosion in the television

19.2: /ʒ/   *su*   **Test Word mea*su*re**

casual	leisure	pleasure	usual	visual
enclosure	measure	treasure		

Dictation

1. Measure the size of the enclosure.
2. He found the hidden treasure.
3. As usual she wore casual clothes.

19.3: /ʒ/   *ge*   **Test Word presti*ge***

beige   camouflage   garage   massage   prestige

Dictation

1. They painted the garage beige.

19.4: /ʒ/   *zu*   **Test Word sei*zu*re**

azure   seizure

SECTION 20. /h/   SPELLING ALTERNATIVES

1. **h**eat
2. **wh**ole

20.1: /h/   *h*   **Test Word *h*eat**

Initial			Medial	
hand	hit	hot	behave	inherit
heat	hoof	how	behind	perhaps
hen	hop	hunt	inhale	rehearse
hill	hope			

Dictation

1. The hen went up the hill.
2. Perhaps he will behave if he stays behind.

20.2: /h/   *wh*   **Test Word *wh*ole**

who   whole   wholly   whooping
whoever   whom

Dictation

1. Who ate the whole cake?

AFFRICATES

21. /tʃ/
22. /dʒ/
23. /ts/
24. /ks/
25. /gz/

SECTION 21. /tʃ/   SPELLING ALTERNATIVES

1. **ch**ip
2. **c**at**ch**   4. pi**c**ture
3. **t**une   5. ques**t**ion

21.1: /tʃ/   *ch*   **Test Word *chip***

	Initial			Final
chain	charm	cheek	chip	bunch
chair	chase	cheese	chop	lunch
chalk	chat	chick	church	much
chance	cheap	child		rich
change	check	chimney		such

Dictation

1. The child sat on the chair in the church.
2. We had chops, chips and cheese for lunch.
3. He is such a rich man he has so much money.

21.2: /tʃ/   *tch*   **Test Word ca*tch***

After /æ/ /ɛ/ /ɪ/ /ɒ/ and /ʌ/ (short vowels) write t before ch

/æ/	/ɛ/	/ɪ/	/ɒ/	/ʌ/
batch	fetch	bitch	scotch	dutch
catch	ketchup	hitch		
hatch	sketch	kitchen		
latch	stretch	switch		
match		witch		
scratch				
thatch				

Note /ɒ/ watch

Dictation

1. Fetch the match from the kitchen.
2. Close the latch on the rabbit hutch.
3. Watch me catch the ball.

21.3: /tʃ/   *t* (u)   **Test Word *tune***

actual	tube	tuition	tuna	tunic
factual	tudor	tulip	tune	tutor
tuba	Tuesday			

Dictation

1. Play a tune on the tuba.
2. I see my tutor on Tuesdays.

21.4: /tʃ/   *tu* (re)   **Test Word pic*ture***

adventure	denture	literature	nature	stature
capture	fixture	manufacture	picture	structure
creature	future	mixture	puncture	venture
culture	lecture			

Dictation

1. It was an adventure to capture the creature.
2. He drew pictures of furniture.

21.5: /tʃ/   *ti* (on)   **Test Word ques*ti*on**

question   suggestion

Dictation

1. It was my suggestion to ask that question.

SECTION 22. /dʒ/   SPELLING ALTERNATIVES

1. **j**ump
2. bri**dge**
3. ma**g**ic
4. **d**uties
5. a**dj**ective

22.1: /dʒ/   *j*   **Test Word *j*ump**

enjoy	jazz	jig	jolly	jumper
Jack	jean	Jim	jot	June
jacket	jeep	jitter	journey	jungle
jam	jelly	jive	judge	junk
Jane	jerk	job	judo	majesty
Japan	jest	jog	jug	major
jar	jet	John	juice	majority
jaw	jew	join	July	perjury
jay	jewel	joke	jump	prejudice

Dictation

1. Jack took the jar of jam.
2. John jogs to his job.
3. Jim and Jane jump in the jeep.

22.2: /dʒ/   *dge*   **Test Word bri*dge***

After /æ/ /ɛ/ /ɪ/ /ɒ/ and /ʌ/ (short vowels) write d before ge

/æ/	/ɛ/	/ɪ/	/ɒ/	/ʌ/
badge	edge	bridge	dodge	budget
badger	hedge	fridge	lodge	fudge
cadge	ledge	midget	podge	grudge
	pledge	ridge	podgy	judge
	sledge		stodge	smudge
	wedge			trudge

Dictation

1. The podgy judge ate fudge from the fridge.
2. The badger sat on the edge of the bridge.
3. Sledge along the ridge and stop at the edge of the ledge.

22.3: /dʒ/   *g*   **Test Word magic**

g followed by e, i or y makes the /dʒ/ sound (soft g).

ge	-age	gi	gy
age	average	agile	biology
general	courage	fragile	Egypt
gel	damage	giant	energy
gem	encourage	gin	geology
genius	forage	ginger	gymnastics
gent	garbage	giraffe	gypsy
gentle	homage	gist	gyro
George	luggage	logic	theology
germ	manage	magic	
German	package	rigid	
legend	plumage		
page	rummage		
rage	sausage		
tragedy	savage		
	scrummage		
	village		

Note: suggest exaggerate

Dictation

1. George was in a rage when he lost his baggage in Germany.
2. The gentle general was a legend in the village.
3. The magic giant drank gin.
4. We need energy to do gymnastics.

22.4: /dʒ/ *d* before a vowel Test Word *duties*

dual	duet	durable	duty	gradual
dubious	dew	during	endure	pendulum
due	duke	dutiful	educate	soldier
duel				

Dictation

1. The duke sang a duet with the soldier.

22.5: /dʒ/   *dj*   **Test Word a*dj*ective**

adjacent	adjective	adjoin	adjudicate	adjust

Dictation

1. An adjective describes a noun.
2. She will adjudicate an exam tomorrow.

SECTION 23. /ts/   SPELLING ALTERNATIVES

1. schizoid

23.1: /ts/   *z*   **Test Word schizoid**

scherzo   schizoid   schizophrenia

Dictation

1. She played the scherzo beautifully.
2. He was suffering from schizophrenia.

SECTION 24. /ks/   SPELLING ALTERNATIVES

1. box   3. exception
2. expand   4. accessible

24.1: /ks/   *x*   **Test Word box**

Final

box	lax	ox	six	vex
fix	mix	sex	tax	wax
fox				

Dictation

1. Fix the box for the fox.   2. Mix up the six sweets.

24.2: /ks/   *x*   **Test Word expand**

Medial

axis	exclude	exit	export	extraordinary
axle	excuse	expand	express	extravagant
exchange	exercise	expect	extent	Oxford
exclaim	exhaust	expensive	extinct	oxygen
exclosure	exhibit	explain	extra	

Dictation

1. It is expensive to export oxygen.
2. We did exactly the same exam.
3. He made excuses not to exercise.

24.3: /ks/   *xc*   **Test Word *exception***

exceed	excell	except	exception
excess	excellent		

Dictation

1. His work was excellent except he always made spelling mistakes.

24.4: /ks/   *cc*   **Test Word *accessible***

access   accessible   accident   success   vaccinate

Dictation

1. He was vaccinated after the accident.

SECTION 25. /gz/   SPELLING ALTERNATIVES

1. exact

25.1: /gz/   *x*   **Test Word *exact***

exact	exactly	exam	example	exasperate
exist				

Dictation

1. He was a good example to his younger brothers.
2. Her mother got exasperated when she was naughty.

FRICTIONLESS CONTINUANTS

26. /l/
27. /r/
28. /w/
29. /j/

SECTION 26. /l/   SPELLING ALTERNATIVES

1. low
2. dwell
3. cycle
4. animal

26.1: /l/   **Test Word *low***

Initial

lace	land	leg	line	long
lack	lap	lend	lip	look
lad	late	less	list	lot
lady	lead	let	live	love
lake	leaf	lid	lock	low
lamb	leap	lie	loft	luck
lame	left	like		

Dictation

1. The lad had a lot of luck.
2. Let the lady look at the loft.

26.2: /l/   *ll*   **Test Word dwe*ll***

After   /ɔ/   /ɛ/   /ɪ/   /ʌ/   /ʊ/   /æ/   /ɒ/   (short vowels) and /əʊ/ write ll.

/ɔ/	/ɛ/	/ɪ/	/ʌ/	/ʊ/
all	bell	bill	dull	bull
ball	fell	drill	gull	full
call	sell	fill	hull	pull
fall	shell	frill	lull	
hall	smell	grill	mull	
small	spell	hill		
tall	tell	ill		
wall	well	kill		
	yell	mill		
		pill		
		spill		
		thrill		
		till		

/æ/	/ɒ/	/əʊ/
shall	doll	droll
		knoll
		poll
		roll
		scroll
		stroll
		toll
		troll

Dictation

1. The ball went over the tall wall.
2. You can spell very well.
3. Shall we ring the bell?

26.3: /l/   *le*   **Test Word cyc*le***

ble	ple	dle	tle
able	ample	candle	battle
bible	apple	handle	cattle
bubble	cripple	idle	kettle
hobble	crumple	ladle	little
humble	dimple	middle	nettle
noble	example	muddle	settle
pebble	people	needle	title
possible	purple	poodle	
stable	simple	saddle	
stumble	steeple		
table	topple		

gle	cle	fle	zle
angle	article	muffle	dazzle
bangle	buckle	rifle	embezzle
bugle	circle	trifle	puzzle
eagle	cycle	truffle	sizzle
giggle	freckle		
single	tackle		
struggle	tickle		
	uncle		

Dictation

1. Put the single candle in the middle of the table.
2. The horse stumbled on the pebbles and hobbled to the stable.
3. You will topple if you don't sit in the middle of the saddle.

26.4: /l/   *al*, **el, il, ol, ual**   **Test Word anim*al***

Do not write le after s, (+ soft c), m, n, r, v or w.

al	el	il	ol	ual
animal	camel	April	control	actual
brutal	cancel	pencil	enrol	equal
decimal	funnel	peril		gradual
dismal	jewel	stencil		individual
final	kennel			manual
funeral	novel			mutual
naval	panel			usual
original	towel			
signal	travel			
	tunnel			
	vowel			

Dictation

1. The brutal animal killed its rival.
2. I bought a novel about travel.
3. The dog dug a tunnel under the kennel.
4. I can not control my pencil.
5. It is usual for the gears to be manual.

SECTION 27. /r/   SPELLING ALTERNATIVES

1. **r**oll
2. **wr**ist
3. **rh**ino

27.1: /r/   *r*   **Test Word** *roll*

(rr in the middle of a
word after a short vowel)

Initial		Medial	rr
rag	rim	bury	barrow
rail	rip	daring	carry
rain	ripe	firing	ferry
ran	road	fury	hurry
rank	rock	hiring	lorry
rat	rod	jury	merry
read	roll	various	narrow
red	roof	wearing	sorry
rest	rope		worry
	rub		

Dictation

1. The rat ran on the red roof in the rain.
2. The crab ran under a rock.

27.2: /r/   *wr*   **Test Word** *wrist*

wrap	wrench	wriggle	write	writhe
wreath	wrestle	wring	writing	wrong
wreck	wretch	wrinkle	wrote	wrought
wren	wretched	wrist		

Dictation

1. He wrenched his wrist when he wrestled with the wretch.

27.3: /r/   *rh*   **Test Word** *rhino*

rhapsody	rhinoceros	rhubarb	rhyme	rhythm
rhino	Rhodes			

Dictation

1. The rhyme was about a rhino eating rhubarb in Rhodes.

SECTION 28. /w/   SPELLING ALTERNATIVES

1. **w**ant
2. **wh**ere
3. **o**nce
4. s**ue**de

28.1: /w/   *w*   Test Word *want*
(See /ɒ/)

want	way	went	wine	wood
was	we	west	wise	wool
watch	weep	wide	wolf	word
wax	well	win	won	work

Dictation

1. The wise wolf was in the wood.
2. He went to work in the west.
3. We will win some wine.

28.2: /w/   *wh*   Test Word *where*

whale	where	whilst	whisk	whist
what	whether	whine	whisker	whistle
wheat	which	whinny	whiskey	white
wheel	whiff	whip	whisky	whizz
wheeze	while	whirl	whisper	why
when				

Dictation

1. Where is the white wheel?
2. He whined and whimpered when he didn't get his own way.
3. He whistled while he whisked the eggs.

28.3: /w/   *o*

once   one

28.4: /w/   *u*

suede

SECTION 29. /j/   SPELLING ALTERNATIVES

1. yard
2. opinion

29.1: /j/   *y*   **Test Word *yard***

yacht	yell	yet	yolk	your
yard	yellow	yew	you	youth
year	yelp	yesterday	York	yo-yo
yeast	yes	yield	young	

Quiz

1. A colour   = y_____.
2. Opposite of no   = y____.
3. Shout   = y_____.
4. Used to make bread = y_____.
5. The day before today = y_____.
6. Part of an egg   = y_____.
7. Opposite of old   = y_____.

29.2: /j/   *i*   **Test Word *opinion***

billion	convenient	million	opinion	Spaniard
brilliant	dominion	onion	senior	union
companion	familiar			

Dictation

1. It is my opinion that my companion is brilliant.
2. The Spaniard grew a million onions.

CONSONANT BLENDS

INITIAL CONSONANT BLENDS

1. **sp**
spade
spark
spell
spin
spit
spoon
sport
spot

2. **st**
stand
star
stare
stay
step
stick
still
stop

3. **sm**
smack
small
smart
smell
smile
smoke

4. **sn**
snake
snap
sniff
snip
snow

5. **sl**
slam
slap
sleep
slide
slim
slime
slip
slow
slum
sly

6. **sw**
swam
swap
sweat
sweep
sweet
swim
swing
Swiss

7. **sc**
scar
scarf
scooter
scold
Scot

8. **sk**
skate
ski
skill
skim
skip
skirt
skull
sky

9. **spl**
splash
splendid
split

10. **spr**
sprat
spread
spree
spring
sprint

11. **scr**
scrap
scrape
scratch
scream
screen
screw
scribble
script
scrub

12. **str**
strap
straw
stream
stretch
strict
strike
string
strip
stroke
strong

13.	**shr**	shred	14.	**tr**	track	15.	**tw**	twelve
		shriek			train			twenty
		shrimp			tramp			twig
		shrink			trap			twin
		shrub			tree			twist
		shrug			trick			twit
					trim			
					trip			
					troop			
					trunk			
					trust			
					truth			
					try			

16.	**dr**	drag	17.	**dw**	dwarf	18.	**pl**	place
		dragon			dwell			plain
		drain			dwindle			plan
		dream						plane
		drink						planet
		drive						plant
		droop						play
		drop						plop
		drum						plot
		dry						plug
								plum
								plus

19.	**pr**	pram	20.	**br**	brake	21.	**bl**	black
		pray			branch			blade
		press			brand			blame
		pretty			brass			blank
		price			brave			blast
		prince			bread			blind
		prize			break			blink
		prompt			brick			blood
		prove			bride			blot
		proof			bright			blue
		prop			broom			blunt
					brother			
					brush			

22.	**cl**	claim	23.	**cr**	crab	24.	**gl**	glad
		clan			cricket			glade
		clap			crisp			gland
		clasp			crook			glare
		class			crop			glass
		claw			cross			gleam
		clay			crowd			glen
		clean			crown			glide
		clear			crush			globe
		click			cry			gloom
		climb						glory
		clip						glove
		clock						glow
		close						glue
		cloth						
		club						
		clue						

25.	**gr**	gram	26.	**fl**	flab	27.	**fr**	frame
		graze			flag			Frank
		grease			flake			free
		Greece			flame			French
		greedy			flat			fresh
		green			flap			Friday
		grill			flash			fridge
		grim			fleck			friend
		grin			flesh			from
		grind			flew			frost
		grit			floor			fruit
		groan			flower			fry
		ground			fly			
		grub						

28.	**thr**	thread
		three
		threw
		throat
		throb
		through
		thrush

FINAL CONSONANT BLENDS

1. **-st**	2. **-sk**	3. **-sp**
fast	ask	crisp
fist	desk	lisp
first	dusk	wisp
last	flask	
list	mask	
lost	musk	
mast	risk	
mist	whisk	
must		
past		
pest		
rest		
test		
wrist		

4. **-nk**	5. **-nd**	6. **-nt**
bank	and	bent
blank	band	grant
clink	bend	grunt
drink	bond	lent
drunk	find	plant
ink	fund	sent
junk	hand	went
pink	pond	
plonk	sand	
sank	spend	
shrink	stand	
sunk	wind	
tank	wound	
trunk		

7. **-nch**	8. **-mp**	9. **-ct**
bench	camp	act
branch	clamp	exact
bunch	cramp	expect
crunch	damp	fact
drench	dump	pact
lunch	imp	respect
munch	lump	tact
punch	jump	
winch	lamp	
	pump	
	stamp	
	stump	
	tramp	
	trump	

10. **-ft** craft
            croft
            daft
            draft
            drift
            gift
            lift
            rift
            shift
            swift

11. **-lk** bulk
            hulk
            milk
            silk
            whelk

12. **-lp** help
            scalp
            yelp

13. **-ld** bald
            bold
            cold
            child
            fold
            gold
            hold
            mild
            mould
            old
            sold
            wild

14. **-thm** rhythm

15. **-sm** prism

16. **-xt** next
            text
            pretext

GRAMMAR (MORPHOLOGY)

SECTION 1.   VERBS PAST TENSE (ed)

Pronunciation of ed past endings depends on the last sound made before the past ending is added. If the last sound is a d or t then the ed is pronounced /ɪd/. If the last sound is voiced, then the ed is pronounced /d/ and if if the last sound is voiceless, the ed is pronounced /t/

1.1: /ɪd/   **word + ed**

Test Word
waited

act - acted	hound - hounded
aid - aided	land - landed
bond - bonded	mend - mended
delight - delighted	need - needed
distract - distracted	plead - pleaded
end - ended	raid - raided
hand - handed	want - wanted
hunt - hunted	

Dictation

1. We were delighted he wanted to come.
2. The man mended the car.
3. She acted in a new play.

1.2: /d/   Words ending with silent e, drop the e and add ed.

Test Word
saved

accuse - accused	move - moved
advise - advised	oppose - opposed
arrive - arrived	pine - pined
believe - believed	please - pleased
compose - composed	prove - proved
confuse - confused	rage - raged
dare - dared	relieve - relieved
declare - declared	revise - revised
file - filed	save - saved
judge - judged	scare - scared
love - loved	serve - served
manage - managed	surprise - surprised

Dictation

1. She was pleased and surprised when he managed to win the race.
2. He produced a witness who proved he had been wrongly accused.

Test Word
played

1.3: /d/   Voiced word-ending + ed

annoy - annoyed	fail - failed
allow - allowed	fear - feared
appear - appeared	fill - filled
betray - betrayed	perform - performed
clean - cleaned	play - played
complain - complained	refrain - refrained
cream - creamed	remain - remained
delay - delayed	reveal - revealed
deliver - delivered	saw - sawed
destroy - destroyed	seem - seemed
discover - discovered	stay - stayed
exclaim - exclaimed	train - trained
explain - explained	

Dictation

1. She complained that he had not cleaned his room.
2. The children stayed behind and played in the garden.
3. The trained chimps performed in the zoo.

Test Word
helped

1.4: /t/   Voiceless word-ending + ed

abolish - abolished	press - pressed
bluff - bluffed	reach - reached
help - helped	sniff - sniffed
kiss - kissed	talk - talked
miss - missed	thank - thanked
mock - mocked	walk - walked
peep - peeped	wash - washed
preach - preached	wish - wished
	work - worked

Dictation

1. He wished he worked at home.
2. When he reached the airport he found he had missed his plane.

Test Word
liked

1.5: /t/   Words ending with silent e,
                      drop the e and add ed.

commence - commenced	like - liked
converse - conversed	place - placed
escape - escaped	produce - produced
hope - hoped	poke - poked
introduce - introduced	rake - raked

Dictation

1. She hoped he had not escaped from prison.
2. He liked to be introduced to new people.

Test Word
faded

1.6: /ɪd/   Words ending with silent e,
                       drop the e and add ed.

complete - completed	fade - faded
create - created	hate - hated
decide - decided	provide - provided
delude - deluded	reside - resided
divide - divided	translate - translated
excite - excited	wade - waded
exude - exuded	

Dictation

1. She decided she hated her job.

Test Word
hopped

1.7: See Suffix 1

After a short vowel double the
final consonant before adding ed.

fib - fibbed	plan - planned
fit - fitted	plod - plodded
grab - grabbed	scan - scanned
hug - hugged	sip - sipped
jam - jammed	skip - skipped
knit - knitted	tap - tapped
map - mapped	trap - trapped
mop - mopped	trip - tripped
nip - nipped	vet - vetted
pat - patted	wag - wagged

Dictation

1. The dog wagged his tail when he was patted and hugged.
2. She knitted a jumper.
3. He tripped when he skipped down the steps.

Test Word
1.8: See Suffix 7   **y - ied**   *hurried*

> Words ending with a consonant
> followed by y; change the y
> to i and add ed.

accompany - accompanied
apply - applied
bury - buried
carry - carried
copy - copied
cry - cried
deny - denied
dirty - dirtied
empty - emptied
fry - fried
hurry - hurried
imply - implied
intensify - intensified

marry - married
occupy - occupied
pity - pitied
qualify - qualified
rely - relied
reply - replied
satisfy - satisfied
spy - spied
study - studied
supply - supplied
try - tried
worry - worried

Dictation

1. He applied for a new job when he qualified.
2. They got married last week.
3. The teacher was satisfied that he had studied and tried hard in his exam.

Test Word
1.9: /t/   The following irregular verbs add t: *slept*

bend - bent
burn - burnt
creep - crept
deal - dealt
dream - dreamt
feel - felt
keep - kept
kneel - knelt

lean - leant (or leaned)
leap - leapt (or leaped)
mean - meant
sleep - slept
smell - smelt
spell - spelt (or spelled)
spill - spilt (or spilled)
sweep - swept

Note: "ee" words become "e" (/ɛ/), "ea" words remain "ea".

Dictation

1. He knelt down and swept the floor.
2. The room smelt when she spilt the perfume.
3. He dreamt that the house burnt down.

1.10: /d/   The following irregular verbs add d: **e.g. *heard***

hear - heard
say - said
tell - told

Dictation

1. I heard what Tom said when he told her the good news.

SECTION 2.   VERBS - CONTINUOUS

Test Word

2.1:   *ing*   *drinking*

Words with a long vowel sound or ending
with two consonants simply add "ing".

aim - aiming	lick - licking
bleed - bleeding	limp - limping
boil - boiling	lisp - lisping
build - building	meet - meeting
clean - cleaning	mend - mending
climb - climbing	need - needing
cramp - cramping	pass - passing
creep - creeping	rain - raining
drink - drinking	reach - reaching
dust - dusting	snatch - snatching
eat - eating	stand - standing
end - ending	steep - steeping
fight - fighting	spend - spending
find - finding	swell - swelling
float - floating	talk - talking
fuss - fussing	thank - thanking
grasp - grasping	think - thinking
hand - handing	touch - touching
hold - holding	trust - trusting
hunt - hunting	watch - watching
jump - jumping	whizz - whizzing
kill - killing	wind - winding
laugh - laughing	

Dictation

1. The fat man loves eating and drinking.
2. He was limping and his foot was bleeding.

2.2: *ing*

Words ending with silent e, drop the e
and add "ing".

arrange - arranging	love - loving
become - becoming	make - making
bite - biting	pave - paving
choose - choosing	poke - poking
come - coming	please - pleasing
complete - completing	prove - proving
dive - diving	race - racing
drive - driving	ride - riding
face - facing	rise - rising
fade - fading	rule - ruling
freeze - freezing	scare - scaring
give - giving	shake - shaking
have - having	strike - striking
hide - hiding	smoke - smoking
hope - hoping	take - taking
joke - joking	use - using
leave - leaving	weave - weaving
live - living	write - writing

Dictation

1. His fast driving was scaring.
2. I am leaving tomorrow.

Test Word
swimming

2.3:   *ing*

> After a short vowel, double the final
> consonant and add "ing".

bet - betting
bid - bidding
chat - chatting
chip - chipping
clap - clapping
dig - digging
drip - dripping
fit - fitting
forget - forgetting
get - getting
grab - grabbing
grin - grinning
hop - hopping
hit - hitting
knit - knitting
let - letting
mop - mopping
net - netting
pat - patting

plan - planning
plug - plugging
pot - potting
quit - quitting
rot - rotting
run - running
scan - scanning
shop - shopping
ship - shipping
skip - skipping
sit - sitting
spin - spinning
stop - stopping
swim - swimming
tap - tapping
trap - trapping
trip - tripping
vet - vetting
wag - wagging

Dictation

1. She went running and swimming to keep fit.
2. She was sitting knitting a jumper.

Test Word
carrying

2.4:   *ing*

> Words ending with y, simply add "ing".

annoy - annoying
apply - applying
bury - burying
carry - carrying
convey - conveying
copy - copying
delay - delaying
deny - denying
destroy - destroying
envy - envying
ferry - ferrying
fly - flying
hurry - hurrying
marry - marrying

obey - obeying
occupy - occupying
play - playing
pray - praying
qualify - qualifying
rely - relying
reply - replying
satisfy - satisfying
say - saying
stay - staying
sway - swaying
try - trying
worry - worrying

Dictation

1. The puppy was playing with a ball.
2. David was worrying about his test.
3. The plane is flying to Spain.

2.5:   *ing*

Test Word
agreeing

Words ending with ee simply add ing

agree - agreeing   free - freeing
flee - fleeing   see - seeing

Dictation

1. Peter is seeing his sister tomorrow.
2. Martin is agreeing with me.

2.6:   *ing*

Test Word
tying

Words ending with ie, change ie to y
and add "ing".

die - dying   tie - tying
lie - lying   vie - vying

Dictation

1. The cat was lying in its basket.
2. She was tying up her laces.

2.7:   *ing*

Test Word
singeing

The following words do not drop silent e
before adding ing in order to keep the
/d_3/ sound.

binge - bingeing   singe - singeing

SECTION 3.   PLURALS

Test Word
3.1:   *s*   *shoes*

Add the "s" suffix to make the following
words plural.

bedroom(s)	gun(s)	rat(s)
book(s)	hat(s)	river(s)
boy(s)	hill(s)	school(s)
bucket(s)	idea(s)	shoe(s)
cat(s)	jar(s)	skirt(s)
chair(s)	key(s)	toe(s)
cinema(s)	kite(s)	toy(s)
day(s)	lamp(s)	valley(s)
dog(s)	monkey(s)	wig(s)
donkey(s)	mouth(s)	yacht(s)
drawer(s)	pen(s)	zoo(s)
garden(s)	pencil(s)	

Test Words
3.2:   *es*   *boxes, churches*

Words ending with s, sh, ch or x add the
"es" suffix to make the plural.

ass(es)	bush(es)	arch(es)	box(es)
bus(es)	brush(es)	church(es)	fox(es)
cross(es)	dish(es)	crutch(es)	tax(es)
dress(es)	wish(es)	match(es)	
glass(es)		patch(es)	
kiss(es)		scratch(es)	
		stitch(es)	
		watch(es)	
		witch(es)	

Dictation

1. She went on two buses to get the dresses.
2. Wash the dishes with soapy brushes.
3. The witches fell in the ditches and needed crutches.
4. The foxes slept in the boxes.

3.3:   *ves*   **Test Word** *wolves*

Words ending with f or fe change f to v
and add "es" to make the plural:

calf - calves	scarf - scarves
elf - elves	self - selves
half - halves	sheaf - sheaves
knife - knives	shelf - shelves
leaf - leaves	thief - thieves
life - lives	wife - wives
loaf - loaves	wolf - wolves

Dictation

1. The thieves stole the scarves from the shelves.
2. The wolves chased the calves.

ves or s

The following words can either change the
f to v and add es, or just add s:

dwarf	roof	wharf
hoof		

s

The following words just add "s":

chief(s)	handkerchief(s)	waif(s)
gulf(s)	oaf(s)	

3.4:   *ies*   **Test Word** *duties*

Words ending with a consonant followed by
y - change y to i and add "es":

army - armies	fairy - fairies
baby - babies	family - families
berry - berries	jelly - jellies
body - bodies	lady - ladies
city - cities	lorry - lorries
company - companies	mystery - mysteries
copy - copies	party - parties
country - countries	penny - pennies
dairy - dairies	pony - ponies
daisy - daisies	puppy - puppies
diary - diaries	query - queries
duty - duties	ruby - rubies
enemy - enemies	story - stories
entry - entries	supply - supplies
factory - factories	

Dictation

1. The families had puppies and ponies.
2. The ladies drove lorries to the factories.

3.5:   *os*

Test Word
pianos

Words ending with "o" which add the suffix
"s" to make the plural:

banjo(s)	eskimo(s)	solo(s)
curio(s)	piano(s)	soprano(s)
dynamo(s)	radio(s)	

Dictation

1. The eskimos heard the banjos and pianos on the radios.

3.6:   *oes*

Test Word
tomatoes

Words ending with "o" which add the suffix
"es" to make the plural:

buffalo(es)	mosquito(es)	tomato(es)
cargo(es)	motto(es)	torpedo(es)
echo(es)	negro(es)	volcano(es)
hero(es)	potato(es)	

Dictation

1. The cargoes of tomatoes and potatoes arrived at the port.

3.7:   *es*

Test Word
crises

Words ending with "is" or "ix" drop the "is" or
"ix" and add the "es" suffix to make the plural.

analysis - analyses	hypothesis - hypotheses
axis - axes	metamorphosis - metamorphoses
basis - bases	oasis - oases
crisis - crises	thesis - theses

SECTION 4. ADVERBS

4.1: /li/   *ly*

word + ly

anxious(ly)	foolish(ly)	poor(ly)
bad(ly)	glad(ly)	proud(ly)
cheap(ly)	hard(ly)	quick(ly)
clever(ly)	kind(ly)	quiet(ly)
coy(ly)	loud(ly)	suddenly(ly)
crisp(ly)	mild(ly)	sweet(ly)
dark(ly)	month(ly)	tight(ly)
drab(ly)	odd(ly)	willing(ly)
fair(ly)	patient(ly)	

Choose an appropriate adverb from the above list
to describe these verbs, and put them into sentences.

run	sing	write
work	wait	shout

4.2: /li/   *ly*

Do not drop silent e before adding ly.

brave(ly)	immediate(ly)	safe(ly)
fine(ly)	late(ly)	sure(ly)
fortunate(ly)	love(ly)	wide(ly)
home(ly)	name(ly)	wise(ly)

Dictation

1. The army marched bravely into battle.
2. Fortunately the train left immediately we arrived.

Test Word
4.3: /li/   *ily*   *lazily*

Words ending with y, change y to i and add ly.

angry - angrily	hungry - hungrily
body - bodily	lucky - luckily
clumsy - clumsily	merry - merrily
day - daily	noisy - noisily
easy - easily	pretty - prettily
funny - funnily	ready - readily
gay - gaily	steady - steadily
greedy - greedily	shabby - shabbily
happy - happily	weary - wearily
hearty - heartily	

Choose an appropriate adverb from the above list
to describe these verbs and put them into sentences.

lifted	ate	played
dressed	walked	

Test Word
4.4: /li/   *ly*   *simply*

Words ending with le, drop the le and add ly.

bubble - bubbly	muddle - muddly
comfortable - comfortably	noble - nobly
dimple - dimply	pebble - pebbly
feeble - feebly	possible - possibly
freckle - freckly	probable - probably
gentle - gently	sensible - sensibly
giggle - giggly	simple - simply
horrible - horribly	sizzle - sizzly
humble - humbly	suitable - suitably
idle - idly	terrible - terribly
miserable - miserably	tickle - tickly

Note: due - duly
               eerie - eerily
               true - truly
               whole - wholly

Dictation

1. Susan is terribly giggly today.
2. Simon has a freckly face.
3. The beach will probably be pebbly.

4.5: /li/ *ly*

Words ending with l, add ly.

accidental(ly)	gradual(ly)	mental(ly)
actual(ly)	grateful(ly)	practical(ly)
annual(ly)	hopeful(ly)	scornful(ly)
brutal(ly)	individual(ly)	skilful(ly)
careful(ly)	loyal(ly)	truthful(ly)
equal(ly)	manual(ly)	usual(ly)
fatal(ly)		

Note: full - fully
shrill - shrilly

Dictation

1. Robert accidentally broke the glass.
2. We had a school play annually.
3. Sally checked her homework carefully.

4.6: /li/ *ally*

Words ending with ic, add ally.

athletic(ally)	energetic(ally)	physic(ally)
artistic(ally)	fantastic(ally)	scientific(ally)
basic(ally)	frantic(ally)	terrific(ally)
comic(ally)	horrific(ally)	topic(ally)
domestic(ally)	logic(ally)	tropic(ally)
electric(ally)	magic(ally)	

Note: public - publicly

Dictation

1. Mike danced energetically.
2. He carried out the experiment scientifically.
3. Jane ran athletically round the track.

SECTION 5.   PREFIXES

(added to the beginning of a root word to change the meaning)

5.1:   *dis*

Test Words
*dis*comfort
*dis*semble

Meaning: apart away or not

disability	discolour	disorientate
disaccord	disconnect	displace
disadvantage	discontent	disqualify
disagree	discount	dissatisfy
disappear	disgrace	dissemble
disappoint	dishonour	dissertation
disapprove	disinfect	dissident
disbelieve	disjoint	dissipate
discharge	dislike	dissolve
disclaim	disobedient	dissuade
disclose	disorder	

Add the dis prefix and use the words in a sentence.

advantage	approve	like
agree	content	qualify
appear	infect	satisfy

5.2:   *mis*

Test Word
*mis*fortune

Meaning: bad or wrong

misadventure	mislead	misstate
misbehave	misnomer	misstep
misconduct	misread	mistake
misfire	misshape	mistrust
misgovern	misspell	
misinform	misspend	

Add the mis prefix and use the words in sentences.

behave	inform	trust
conduct	spell	

5.3:   *fore*

Test Word
*fore*head

Meaning: in front, before

forearm	forefather	forejudge
forebode	forefinger	foreman
forecast	foreground	foremost
forecourt	forehead	

5.4:   *for*   **Test Word**
                                                              forgo

Meaning: away (forgive)
          prohibition (forbid)
          neglect (forsake)

forbear	forgive	forsake
forbid	forgo	forswear
forget	forlorn	

5.5:   *in*   **Test Word**
                                                            indistinct

Meaning: negative

inaccessible	incomprehensible	innumerable
inaccurate	inconsistency	innutritious
inactive	incorrect	insane
inadequate	independent	insincere
inappropriate	indirect	invisible
inarticulate	inexperience	
incapable	inexpensive	

Add the in prefix and use the words in sentences.

| active | capable | expensive |
| appropriate | dependent | visible |

5.6:   *un*

Meaning: negative

uncommon	unnamed	unreliable
unfriendly	unnatural	unsteady
unfortunate	unnecessary	untrue
unhappy	unnerve	unwilling
unkind	unpopular	

5.7:   *im*
(assimilated form of in - before initial m + p)

Meaning: negative

immaterial	immortal	improbable
immature	impatient	impure
immoral	impossible	

Test Word

5.8:   *ac*   *account*

Meaning: change into, addition

acclaim	accommodate	account
acclimatise	accompany	accredit
		accumulate

Test Word

5.9:   *ir*   *irregular*

Meaning: assimilated form of in - before initial r

irradiate	irregular	irrepressible
irrational	irrelevant	irresponsible
irreconcilable	irreparable	irrigation
irredeemable		

5.10: When words ending with double l are used as a prefix they drop one l (all, full, well, will)

almost	altold	welcome
almighty	already	welfare
also	always	wilful
although	fulfil	
altogether	fulsome	

Note: all right   dullness   fullness

SECTION 6.   SUFFIXES

(an ending added to the end of a root
word to change the grammatical function)

Vowel Suffixes

-able, verb -> noun
-al, adjective
-ed, past tense
-en, adjective
-er, comparative
-es, plural
-est, superlative
-et, nouns
-ing, present participle
-ish, adjective
-ist, verb -> noun
-ive, adjective
-ous, adjective
-y, nouns and adjectives

Consonant Suffixes

-dom - nouns
-ful - adjective
-hood - nouns
-less - adjective and adverbs
-ly - adverbs
-ment - nouns
-ness - adjectives -> noun
-s - plural
-some - adjectives

Test Word
hopped

6.1:

Words ending with a short vowel followed by one
consonant, double the final consonant before adding
vowel suffix.

big: er - est
clap: ed - er - ing
fat: en - er - est - ish - y
hop: ed - er - ing
jam: ed - ing - y
mat: ed - ing
net: ed - er - ing
pat: ed - ing
run: er - ing - y
skip: ed - er - ing
thin: ed - er - est - ing - ish
wet: ed - er - est - ing

If a consonant suffix is added, there is no need to
double.

e.g.,   thin + ly   man + hood
         rim + less   sad + ness

6.2:

e.g. needed

Do not double the final consonant after a long vowel
when adding a vowel suffix.

aid:	ed - ing
aim:	ed - ing
bleed:	ing
cheat:	ed - er - ing
feed:	er - ing
float:	ed - ing
frown:	ed - ing
groan:	ed - er - ing
leak:	ed - ing - y
mow:	ed - ing
need:	ed - ing - y
read:	able - er - ing
show:	ed - ing - y
speak:	er - ing

6.3:

e.g. hunter

Do not double if there are two consonants at the end of
the word when adding a vowel suffix.

act:	ed -or - ing - ive
bind:	er - ing
hold:	er - ing
limp:	ed - er - ing
match:	ed - ing
stamp:	ed - ing
trust:	ed - ing - y
want:	ed - ing

6.4: e.g. *leaving*

Words ending with silent e drop the e before adding a vowel suffix (see Verbs Past Tense 2, 5 & 6; Verbs Continuous 2).

believe: ed - er - ing
choose: ing - y
come: ing
drive: able - er - ing
fade: ed - ing
fame: ed - ous
give: er - ing
hope: ed - er - ing
leave: ing
move: able - ed - er - ing
poke: ed - er - ing
style: ed - ing - ish
wade: ed - er - ing

Test Word
lovely

6.5:

Words ending with one consonant and silent e, keep the e when adding a consonant suffix. (See Adverbs 2).

amaze: ment
blame: less
brave: ly
excite: ment
home: ly - less - lessness
hope: ful - less - lessness
love: ly
move: ment
safe: ly
tire: less - some

6.6:   e.g. *noticeable*

Words ending with ce or ge adding a suffix beginning
with a, o or a consonant - do not drop silent e, in
order to keep the /s/ and /dʒ/ sound.

advance:	ment
advantage:	ous
change:	able - less
courage:	ous
engage:	ment
gorge:	ous
hinge:	less
manage:	able - ment
notice:	able
outrage:	ous
peace:	able - ful
pronounce:	able - ment
service:	able
trace:	able - less

Test Word
lazily

6.7:

Words ending with a consonant followed by y, change the
y to i before adding suffix (except suffixes beginning
with i).

beauty:	ful
bury:	ed
carry:	ed - es
cry:	ed
deny:	ed
easy:	er - est - ly
empty:	ed - er
funny:	er - est - ly
factory:	es
lonely:	er - est - ness
lovely:	er - est - ness
marry:	ed - es
pity:	ed - es - ful
reply:	ed - es - ful
try:	ed - es
ugly:	er - est - ness
worry:	ed - er

6.8*:**   *e.g. **babyish

Words ending with a consonant followed by y, keep the y
when adding a suffix beginning with i (see Verbs
Continuous 4).

baby:	ing - ish
bury:	ing
carry:	ing
early:	ish
hurry:	ing
marry:	ing
occupy:	ing
puppy:	ish
worry:	ing

6.9*:**   *e.g. **delayed

Words ending with a vowel followed by y just add suffix
(see Verbs Past 2, Verbs Continuous 4).

annoy:	ed - ing - s
delay:	ed - ing - s
obey:	ed - ing - s
play:	ed - er - ing - ful - s
say:	ing
stay:	ed - er - s

Test Word
picnicking

***6.10*:**

Words ending with ic add k before adding a vowel suffix
which would soften the c.

colic:	y
frolic:	ed - ing - y
magic:	ed
mimic:	ed - ing
panic:	ed - er - ing - y
picnic:	ed - er - ing
plastic:	y
traffic:	ed - ing

Test Word
wonderful

6.11:

When all full and till are added as a suffix they drop
one l.

bashful	grateful	mournful
beautiful	handful	mouthful
careful	hopeful	powerful
dreadful	houseful	spoonful
forgetful	joyful	wonderful
fulfil	masterful	

Note: until

SECTION 7.   ENDINGS

(differentiated from suffixes in that
they are an integral part of the word)

7.1:   *ible*   Test Word *horrible*

compatible	horrible	perfectible
comprehensible	incredible	permissible
corruptible	intelligible	possible
credible	invincible	responsible
divisible	invisible	terrible
edible	legible	visible
enforcible		

Dictation

1. It is impossible to become invisible.
2. The horrible food did not look edible.

7.2:   *able*   Test Word *capable*

abominable	comfortable	inscrutable
acceptable	educable	liveable
believable	enjoyable	lovable
capable	explicable	noticeable
changeable	impeccable	reliable

Dictation

1. We had an enjoyable holiday, the hotel was very comfortable.
2. The abominable snowman is a lovable creature.

7.3:   *ery*   Test Word *brewery*

brewery	embroidery	machinery
cemetery	grocery	monastery
confectionery	jewellery	nursery
crockery	joinery	stationery
discovery		

Dictation

1. There is an old cemetery at the monastery.
2. The machinery at the brewery was new.

7.4:   *ent*   **Test Word**
                                            impudent

confident   eminent   impudent
convenient   evident   insolent
eloquent   independent

Dictation

1. It was evident that he was confident because he made such an eloquent speech.

7.5:   *ant*   **Test Word**
                                            informant

abundant   elegant   instant
assistant   extravagant   significant
brilliant   ignorant

Dictation

1. She was both elegant and brilliant.

7.6:   *ance*   **Test Word**
                                            hindrance

abundance   elegance   instance
assistance   extravagance   reluctance
brilliance   hindrance   significance
countenance   ignorance

Dictation

1. His ignorance of grammar was a hindrance when he wrote essays.
2. Her extravagance is of no significance.

7.7:   *ence*   **Test Word**
                                            independence

confidence   eloquence   impudence
convenience   eminence   indolence
correspondence   evidence   insolence

Dictation

1. His evidence was given in the strictest confidence.
2. He was expelled from school for his impudence and insolence.

7.8:   *ary*   **Test Word**
                                                temporary

anniversary	January	stationary
contrary	library	summary
dictionary	military	temporary
February	necessary	tributary
honorary	ordinary	voluntary

Dictation

1. Is the anniversary in January or February?
2. He got a dictionary from the library.

7.9:   *ory*   **Test Word**
                                                compulsory

accessory	factory	observatory
category	history	refectory
explanatory	laboratory	territory

Dictation

1. It was compulsory for all the children to study history.
2. The factory had a large laboratory.

7.10:   *ity*   **Test Word**
                                                prosperity

ability	curiosity	prosperity
activity	enormity	punctuality
animosity	generosity	regularity
audacity	mediocrity	sanctity
capacity	necessity	university
celebrity	possibility	

Dictation

1. The celebrity visited the university.
2. His prosperity led to his generosity.

7.11:   *ify*   **Test Word**
                                                specify

beautify	horrify	pacify
clarify	jollify	qualify
deify	lignify	ratify
disqualify	magnify	sanctify
edify	nullify	specify
electrify		

Dictation

1. He will qualify as a doctor next week.
2. He tried to pacify the hysterical woman.

		Test Word
7.12:	*efy*	*liquefy*

liquefy   rarefy   stupefy
putrefy

Anagrams

1. To make into liquid = fiqleuy
2. To rot   = rutpfey

STRESS

1.   *e.g. Galloped*

If the first syllable of a word is stressed, do not double the final consonant before adding a suffix.

alter - altered	lengthen - lengthened
ballot - balloted	limit - limited
budget - budgeting	market - marketing
enter - entered	number - numbered
fasten - fastened	offer - offered
gallop - galloped	orbit - orbiting
hamper - hampered	pocket - pocketing
happen - happened	pivot - pivoting
hasten - hastened	profit - profited
hinder - hindering	

Test Word
2.   *Forbidden*

If the second syllable of a word is stressed, double the final consonant before adding a suffix.

acquit - acquitted	outwit - outwitted
admit - admitted	permit - permitted
begin - beginner	prefer - preferred
commit - committed	propel - propeller
debar - debarred	recur - recurring
equip - equipped	refer - referring
forbid - forbidden	regret - regrettable
outbid - outbidden	

Test Word
3.   *Traveller*

Words ending with l double regardless of stress.

cancel - cancelled	quarrel - quarrelling
compel - compelled	signal - signalled
label - labelled	travel - traveller
pedal - pedalling	

NOTE
except: -ity, -ise/-ize (formality, legalise)

PASSAGES FOR DICTATION

1. After Diagnostic Assessment List 6

Toad fell into the pond. He sank to the bottom and came up again. "Drat," said Toad. "All our sweet, cold ice cream has washed away."

Extract from "The Wind in the Willows" by Kenneth Graham.
Published by Methuen Children's Books Ltd

2. After Diagnostic Assessment List 7

No grass is left on the hill for little goat Gruff to eat and get fat. So Gruff went to the bridge over the water. I can eat the green grass at the end of the bridge.

Extract from "The Three Goats" (The Gayway Series) by E.R Boyce.
Published by Macmillan.

3. After Diagnostic Assessment List 10

Tim had just finished his apple, when he heard a sound like a stick breaking. He jumped to his feet and looked along the path.

A great log lay across the grass. As Tim looked, the log heaved itself slowly upright. Two long, bare branches reached out to bar his way.

Two green eyes opened in the stump, shining under the dead branches.

Extract from "Tim and the Hidden People" by Sheila McCullagh.
Published by E.J. Arnold.

4. After Diagnostic Assessment List 13

Spot ran quickly all the way home where he saw Mum standing on the doorstep, wiping her hands on her yellow apron. She was just wondering where Justin had got to when she saw Spot running across the front lawn barking. "What's the matter, Spot?" said Mum, as Spot carried on barking loudly. Mum realized that Spot wanted her to follow him, and guessing that there had been an accident, she grabbed the red first aid box and followed Spot down the street, running all the way and calling out Justin's name as she went.

Extract from "Extra Biscuits For Spot" by Clare Shaw.
Published by The Alphabet Children Ltd.

5. After Diagnostic Assessment List 14

An ant once leaned too far over the edge of a river and fell into the water. A dove was watching from a tree nearby. She saw that the ant could not swim so she plucked off a leaf and threw it down to him. He just managed to scramble onto it and in time the wind blew him safely to the edge of the water.

Extract from "The Fables of Aesop". Published by Penguin.

6. *After Diagnostic Assessment List 15*

Once again I must stress that what is good for you is not necessarily good for the animal, and what the animal likes is not necessarily what you like.

A fair example of this rule is provided by the case of our colony of African civets. I originally brought back a fine male specimen of this handsome grey and black spotted species from the Cameroons in 1965 and we managed to obtain a mate for him from Uganda.

Extract from "The Stationary Ark" by Gerald Durrell.
Published by Fontana.

7. *After Diagnostic Assessment List 16*

One day when Pooh Bear had nothing else to do he thought he would do something, so he went round to Piglet's house to see what Piglet was doing. It was still snowing as he stumped over the white forest track and he expected to find Piglet warming his toes in front of his fire, but to his surprise he saw that the door was open, and the more he looked inside the more Piglet wasn't there.

Extract from "The House at Pooh Corner" by A.A. Milne.
Published by Methuen Children's Books Ltd.

8. *After Diagnostic Assessment List 17*

There were spooks in there. Jim and Arthur knew this for sure because they had heard the ghostly screams.

Sometimes they dared one another to squeeze through the gate where the bars had rusted away and creep up the overgrown drive. Thick bushes grew on either side dripping and rustling.

Extract from "It's too frightening for me" by Shirley Hughes
Published by Young Puffin.

9. *After Diagnostic Assessment List 18*

And the girl daughter picked him up on the palm of her hand and sat him on the bottom of the canoe and gave him her scissors, and he waved them in his little arms, and opened them and shut them and snapped them and said, "I can eat nuts.

I can crack shells. I can dig holes. I can climb trees. I can breathe the dry air ... I didn't know I was so important."

Extract from "The Crab that Played with the Sea" from The Just So Stories by Rudyard Kipling. Reproduced by kind permission of The National Trust for Places of Historic Interest or Natural Beauty. Published by Macmillan London Ltd

10. *After Diagnostic Assessment List 20*

For the rest of the week, however, they were undisturbed, the only thing that excited any attention being the continual renewal of the blood stain on the library floor. This certainly was very strange, as the door was always locked at night ..... and the windows kept closely barred. The chameleon-like colour, also of the stain excited a good deal of comment.

Extract from "Ghostly and Ghastly" by Barbara Ireson.
Published by Beaver Original.

11. *After Diagnostic Assessment List 22*

But although the senses sometimes deceive us concerning things which are barely perceptible or at a great distance, there are perhaps many other things about which one cannot reasonably doubt, although we know them through the medium of the senses.

Extract from "Discourse on Method and Other Writings" by R. Descartes. Published by Penguin Classics

12. *After Diagnostic Assessment List 23*

When he wasn't asleep Frederick had been friendly enough, though he often laughed loudly for no reason they could see and said things there was no answer to ... this sort of behaviour was tiresome but bearable and as they walked to Druid's Grove, Carrie thought she quite liked him.

Extract from "Carrie's War" by Nina Bawden. Published by Puffin

13. *After Diagnostic Assessment List 26*

Ingenious you certainly were - like monkeys. But you neglected your philosophers to your own ruin. Each new discovery was a toy. You never considered its true worth. You just pushed it into your system - a system already suffering from hardening of the arteries. And you were a greedy people. You took each discovery as if it were a bright new garment, but when you put it on you wore it over your old verminous rag. You had grave need of disinfectants.

Extract from "The Seeds of Time" by John Wyndham. Published by Penguin.

14. After Diagnostic Assessment List 28

There are no well-defined seasons in the jungle and there is therefore no obvious climatic cue for all the trees to shed their leaves simultaneously as there is in other latitudes. But this does not mean that all trees shed and regrow their leaves continuously throughout the year. Each species has its own timing. Some drop leaves every six months. Others do so after what seems to be a quite arbitrary period with no discernible logic in it - every twelve months and twenty-one days, for example. Still others do it piecemeal, at intervals throughout the year a branch at a time.

Extract from "The Living Planet" by David Attenborough.
Published by William Collins.

Word Index

Gnarl 90
Gnash 90
Gnat 90
Gnaw 27,43,89,90
Gnome 90
Gnu 90
Go 63,86
Goal 61,86
Goat 5,61,86
God 86
Gold 62,86,117
Golden 89
Golf 86
Gone 41,86
Good 46,86
Goose 95
Gore 42
Gorgeous 56
Got 40,86
Govern 50,90
Gown 68
Grab 86
Grabbed 120
Grabbing 80,124
Gracious 56,100
Gradual 105,109
Gradually 131
Gram 115
Grammar 54
Grand 86
Grant 116
Graph 93
Graphics 93
Grasp 38,86
Grasping 122
Grass 95
Grate 60
Grateful 140
Gratefully 131
Graze 97,115
Grease 115
Great 59,60
Greece 115
Greedily 130
Greedy 30,115
Green 29,86,115
Grew 48
Grey 58,59
Grief 31
Grieve 31
Grill 108,115
Grim 115
Grin 33,115
Grind 66,115
Grinning 124
Grit 115
Groan 61,64,115
Groaner 136
Groaning 136
Grocery 141
Groom 47
Grotesque 19,82,85
Ground 68,115
Group 49
Grove 94
Grow 62
Growl 68
Grown 62,64
Grub 115
Grudge 104
Gruff 93
Grunt 50,116
Guarantee 86
Guard 86
Guardian 86
Guerilla 86

Guernsey 86
Guess 86,95
Guest 86
Guidance 86
Guide 86
Guild 34,86
Guile 86
Guillotine 86
Guilt 34,86
Guilty 19,25,34,85,86
Guinea 86
Guitar 86
Gulf 86
Gulfs 127
Gull 86,108
Gulp 86
Gum 86,88
Gun 50,86,89
Gunned 89
Guns 126
Gush 86
Gust 86
Gut 86
Gutter 86
Guy 65
Gymnastics 105
Gypsy 33,105
Gyrate 76
Gyro 65,105

Haemoglobin 32
Hair 72
Half 16,25,38,39,92
Hall 42,45,108
Halt 42
Halves 127
Ham 37
Hampered 145
Hand 37,102,116
Handed 118
Handful 140
Handing 122
Handle 109
Hang 91
Handkerchiefs 127
Hanky 83
Happen 19,26,89
Happened 145
Happily 30,130
Happy 30,79
Harangue 91
Harbour 17,27,54,55
Hard 38
Hardly 129
Hare 72
Harm 38,88
Hasten 96
Hastened 145
Hat 5,80
Hatch 103
Hate 58
Hated 120
Hats 126
Haughty 44
Haul 44,45
Haunt 44
Have 19,24,93
Having 123
Hay 59
Head 25,35,82
Heal 32
Health 35
Hear 70,72
Heard 22,53,121
Hearse 53
Heart 16,26,38,39

Hearth 39
Heartily 130
Heat 16,20,24,29,102
Heather 35
Heaven 35
Heavy 35
Hedge 104
Heel 29,32
Heifer 36
Height 66
Heir 72
Heiress 72
Heirloom 72
Help 117
Helped 22,25,119
Hen 89.102
Herb 52
Herbaceous 101
Here 71,72
Hero 63
Heroes 128
Heroic 84
Hid 33,82
Hide 65,82
Hidden 82,89
Hideous 56
Hiding 123
High 66
Higher 54
Hilarious 56
Hill 102,108
Hills 126
Him 88
Hind 66
Hindering 145
Hindrance 23,27,142
Hingeless 138
Hip 79
Hire 76
Hiring 110
Hiss 95
Historic 84
Historically 22,26
History 143
Hit 33,80,102
Hitch 103
Hitting 124
Hoard 45
Hoarse 44
Hobble 109
Hobby 80
Hockey 30
Hoe 63
Hoist 70
Hold 62,117
Holder 136
Holding 122,136
Holy 30
Homage 105
Home 61
Homeless 137
Homelessness 137
Homely 129.137
Honest 16,26,40,41
Honey 30,50
Honorable 41
Honorary 143
Honour 41,55
Honourable 41
Hood 46
Hoof 102
Hoofs 127
Hook 46
Hooves 127
Hop 79,102
Hope 79,102

Hoped 119
Hopeful 140
Hopefully 131
Hoping 123,
Hopped 22,23,25
Hopping 124
Horde 45
Horn 42
Horrible 23,26,141
Horribly 130
Horrifically 131
Horrify 143
Horse 42
Host 62
Hot 40,102
Hotter 80
Hound 68
Hounded 118
Hour 5,18,26,77
House 17,20,25,68,95
Houseful 140
How 68,102
Howl 68
Huff 93
Hug 86
Hugged 120
Hulk 117
Hull 108
Human 90
Humble 109
Humbly 130
Humming 88
Humorous 56
Humour 55
Hung 91
Hunger 92
Hungrily 130
Hunt 50,102
Hunted 118
Hunter 23
Hunting 122
Hurl 52
Hurried 22,25,121
Hurry 30,110
Hurrying 124,139
Hurt 52
Husband 98
Hush 50
Hussar 98
Hustle 96
Hut 50
Hydra 65
Hydrant 65
Hygiene 65
Hymn 33,88
Hyphen 93
Hypnosis 33
Hypotheses 128

Ice 5,65
Ideas 126
Idle 109
Idly 130
Igneous 56
Ignorance 142
Ignorant 142
I'll 68
Ill 108
Immaterial 133
Immature 133
Immediate 57
Immediately 129
Immense 95
Immoral 133
Immortal 133
Imp 116

Ride 65
Ridge 104
Ridiculous 17,27,54,56
Riding 123
Rifle 109
Rift 116
Right 66,68
Rigid 105
Rim 110
Rimmed 88
Rimless 135
Rind 66
Ring 33,91
Rink 91
Rinse 95
Rip 79,110
Ripe 65,79,110
Ripped 79
Rising 123
Risk 110
Rite 68
Rivers 126
Road 61,64,110
Roar 26,44
Roast 61
Rob 80
Robber 54
Rock 84,110
Rod 110
Rode 61,64
Roe 63
Rogue 86
Role 64
Roll 20,25,61,62
64,108,110
Roof 47,110
Roofs 127
Rook 46,83
Room 47
Rope 79,110
Rot 40
Rote 61
Rotten 80,89
Rotting 124
Rough 51,93
Round 68
Route 16,47,49
Row 62
Rowed 64
Roy 69
Royal 69
Rub 110
Rubber 54
Rubies 127
Rude 49
Rug 86
Ruling 123
Rum 88
Rummage 105
Rumour 55
Run 89
Running 89,124,135
Runny 135
Rush 99
Russia 100
Rut 50
Ruth 49

Sabre 55
Sack 84,95
Sad 16,20,24,37,95
Saddle 109
Safe 92
Safely 129,137
Said 16,25,35,36,82,121
Sail 58,60

Sale 58,60
Salt 42
Same 58
Sanctify 143
Sanctity 143
Sand 37,116
Sank 37,83,91,116
Sap 95
Sat 37
Satisfied 121
Satisfy 65
Satisfying 124
Saturday 57
Sauce 44
Saucer 44
Saunter 44
Sausage 41,105
Savage 105
Save 58,94
Saved 22,25,118
Saviour 55
Saw 43,45
Sawed 119
Say 95
Saying 124,139
Scalp 117
Scanned 120
Scanning 124
Scar 38,113
Scared 118
Scarf 113
Scaring 123
Scarves 127
Scene 97
Scenery 97
Scent 37,97
Sceptre 55,97
Scheme 85
Scherzo 106
Schizoid 5,20,28,85,106
Schizophrenia 85,106
School 47,85
Schools 126
Sciatica 97
Science 20,27,95,97
Scientific 84,97
Scientifically 131
Scientist 97
Scintillate 97
Scissors 97,98
Scold 62,113
Scone 41
Scooter 113
Scope 79
Scornfully 131
Scot 113
Scotch 103
Scout 68
Scrap 79,113
Scrape 113
Scratch 103,113
Scratches 126
Scream 29,113
Screen 113
Screw 16,25,47,48,113
Scribble 113
Script 113
Scroll 108
Scrub 113
Scrummage 105
Scythe 97
Sea 29,32
Seam 32
Search 53
Seat 29,95
Section 99

See 32,95
Seed 29
Seeing 125
Seem 29,32
Seemed 119
Seen 29
Seize 31,97
Seizure 20,28,31,101,102
Selection 99
Sell 108
Selves 127
Senior 112
Sense 95
Sensibly 130
Sent 35,37,116
Sepulchre 55
Sergeant 16,28,38,39
Serial 72
Serious 56
Serve 52
Served 118
Serviceable 138
Session 100
Set 35,95
Sett 81
Setting 80
Settle 109
Severe 71
Sew 62,64
Sex 106
Shabbily 130
Shaft 39
Shake 99
Shaken 89
Shaking 123
Shall 99,108
Share 72
Shark 38,99
Sharp 38
Shave 94
Shawl 43
She 99
Sheaves 127
Shed 20,24,98,99
Sheep 29,99
Sheet 29,99
Shell 99,108
Shelves 127
Shepherd 52
Shield 31
Shift 117
Shine 99
Ship 33,99
Shipping 124
Shirt 51,99
Shock 84,99
Shoe 5,48,99
Shoes 16,20,22,25,47
48,97,98,126
Shone 16,26,41
Shoot 99
Shopper 54
Shopping 79,124
Shore 42
Short 42
Shot 80
Should 46
Shoulder 28,61,64
Shove 94
Show 62,99
Showed 136
Shower 77
Showing 136
Showy 136
Shred 114
Shriek 31,114

Shrilly 131
Shrimp 114
Shrink 91,114,116
Shrub 114
Shrug 114
Shut 50
Shy 65
Sick 84
Side 65
Siege 31
Sigh 66
Sight 66,68
Sign 90
Signal 109
Signalled 145
Significance 142
Significant 142
Silk 33,117
Silly 30
Silver 54
Simmer 88
Simple 109
Simply 22,26,130
Simultaneous 56
Sing 33,91
Singeing 22,27,125
Single 92,109
Sings 98
Singular 54
Sink 83
Sip 79
Sipped 120
Sir 51
Sire 76
Sister 54
Sit 33,80,95
Site 68
Sitting 124
Six 106
Sizzle 109
Sizzly 130
Skate 113
Sketch 103
Ski 113
Skilfully 131
Skill 113
Skim 113
Skipped 120,135
Skipper 135
Skipping 124,135
Skirt 51,113
Skirts 126
Skull 113
Sky 65,113
Slam 113
Slap 37,113
Slaughter 44
Slave 94
Sledge 104
Sleep 29,113
Sleigh 60
Slept 22,25,121
Slide 65,113
Slim 33,113
Slime 65,113
Slip 33,113
Slope 61
Slough 69
Slow 62,113
Slug 50
Sluice 49
Slum 113
Sly 65,113
Smack 84,113
Small 42,108,113
Smaller 54

Visual 101
Vogue 86
Voice 70
Volcanoes 128
Vole 94   Volt 94
Voluntary 143
Vote 61
Vow 68
Vowel 68,109
Voyage 69
Vying 125

Waded 120,137
Wader 137
Wading 137
Wagged 120
Wagging 86,124
Waifs 127
Waist 58
Wait 58,60
Waited 25
Waive 58,60
Wake 83
Walk 16,41,43
Walked 119
Wall 42,108
Wand 40
Wander 40
Wane 58
Want 16,20,24,40,111
Wanted 118,136
Wanting 136
War 43
Ward 43
Wares 72
Warm 43
Warp 43
Wart 43
Was 40,111
Wash 40,99
Washed 119
Wasp 40
Watch 5,40,103,111
Watches 126
Watching 122
Watt 81
Wave 60
Wax 106,111
Way 24,58,59,111
We 111
Weak 29
Wealth 35
Weapon 35
Wear 73
Wearily 130
Wearing 110
Weather 35,94
Weaving 123
Web 80
Webbed 80
Wed 82
Wedding 82
Wedge 104
Week 29
Weekly 30
Weep 111
Weight 60
Weir 71
Weird 17,27,70,71
Welcome 134
Welfare 134
Well 108,111
Went 111,116
West 111
Wet 35
Wetted 135

Wetter 135
Wettest 135
Wetting 135
Whale 111
Wharfs 127
Wharves 127
What 40,111
Wheat 29,111
Wheel 29,111
Wheeze 111
Whelk 117
When 111
Where 5,18,20,25,72,111
Whether 94,111
Which 111
Whiff 111
While 111
Whilst 111
Whine 111
Whinny 111
Whip 111
Whipped 79
Whirl 111
Whisk 83,111,116
Whisker 111
Whiskey 111
Whisky 111
Whisper 111
Whist 111
Whistle 96,111
White 111
Whizz 97,111
Whizzing 122
Who 102
Whoever 102
Whole 20,25,102
Wholly 102,130
Whom 102
Whooping 102
Whore 42
Why 65,111
Wide 65,111
Widely 129
Wield 31
Wigs 126
Wild 66,117
Wilful 134
Willingly 129
Win 33,89,111
Winch 116
Wind 33,66,116
Winding 122
Wine 65,111
Wing 5,33,91
Wink 91
Wire 76
Wise 111
Wisely 129
Wiser 54
Wish 99
Wished 119
Wishes 126
Wisp 116
Wit 33
Witches 126
Wives 127
Wizard 54
Woe 63
Wolf 111
Wolves 22,25,127
Woman 90
Womb 88
Women 27,33,34
Won 50,111
Wonder 50
Wonderful 23,25,140

Wood 46,111
Wooden 89
Wool 46,111
Woollen 89
Word 53,111
Wore 42
Work 53,111
Worked 119
World 17,25,53
Worldly 53
Worm 53
Worried 121,138
Worrier 138
Worry 30,50,110
Worrying 124,139
Worse 53
Worship 53
Worth 53
Would 46
Wound 49,68,116
Wrap 110
Wreath 110
Wreck 84,110
Wren 110
Wrench 110
Wrestle 110
Wretch 110
Wretched 110
Wriggle 110
Wring 110
Wrinkle 110
Wrist 20,27,110,116
Write 110
Writhe 110
Writing 110,123
Wrong 110
Wrote 110
Wrought 45,110

Xerox 20,28,97,98
Xylophone 65,98

Yacht 5,112
Yachts 126
Yard 16,20,24,38,112
Yawn 43
Year 70,112
Yeast 112
Yell 108,112
Yellow 112
Yelp 112,117
Yeoman 17,28,61,64
Yes 95,112
Yesterday 112
Yet 80,112
Yew 112
Yield 31,112
Yo-Yo 112
Yoke 64
Yolk 17,61,64,112
York 112
You 49,112
Young 17,26,51,91,112
Your 112
Youth 112

Zany 97
Zeal 97
Zebra 5,97
Zen 97
Zero 71,97
Zigzag 97
Zinc 97
Zip 97
Zither 97
Zodiac 97

Zone 97
Zoo 20,25,97
Zoom 47,97
Zoos 126
Zulu 97